CHURCHILL
at the GALLOP

CHURCHILL
at the GALLOP

Brough Scott

For Hugh

with thanks
for all his
support

November
2017

[signature]

RACING POST

Previous page: WSC rides the Lipizzaner
horse, Salve at Chartwell, October 1946

First published in Great Britain in 2017 by Racing Post Books
27 Kingfisher Court, Hambridge Road, Newbury, Berkshire, RG14 5SJ

10 9 8 7 6 5 4 3 2 1

A catalogue record for this book is available from the British Library.

ISBN 978-1-910497-36-4

Cover image: *Churchill at the Gallop* by Flora Blackett, www.florablackett.com
Designed and typeset by Soapbox, www.soapbox.co.uk

Printed and bound in the Czech Republic by Finidr

To my mother, Irene Florence Scott, 1902–75,
who built sandcastles for Churchill, and who did
much, much more for me

The Battle of Omdurman. A still of Simon
Ward playing WSC in *Young Winston*

INTRODUCTION

By Brough Scott

It is actually pretty difficult to do – and that's if the horse is standing still. Without taking your left hand off the reins, you have to raise your cavalry sword in your right hand across in front of you, and re-sheath it in the scabbard attached to the near side of the saddle. At 8.40 on a steamy hot morning in the Sudan on 2 September 1898, Winston Churchill did it at the gallop. Then he reached forward with the same hand, pulled his Mauser pistol out of its wooden holster and cocked it ready to fire. He needed to. Other bullets were already whistling past him, and 400 yards ahead lay 2,500 pumped-up dervishes intent on cutting him and his fellow cavalrymen to pieces.

Think about it, as I have a lot over the years. In an earlier life I galloped over steeplechase fences for a living, but in the 1965 Grand National there were a mere 47 runners, not 440 Lancers, and at the end of the most hectic ten minutes of my life just three of us were on the way to Walton Hospital, not 22 dying in the desert sand after a similar period of infinitely more frenetic and bloody action. The more you think about it, the tougher it looks.

Like most people who have ever heard about Winston Churchill, and as a war baby his 'Blood, sweat and tears' speech was an accompaniment to my childhood, I sort of knew about the Charge at Omdurman. But, dumbly, it has taken me three score years and ten to consider its equestrian implications. For Churchill to keep his seat as he and his horse crashed into, down, and through the seething, hacking throng in that dried river bed where the main body of the enemy were concealed, took riding skills and dexterity with a pistol almost off the scale. How intense had been his preparation? How much did riding figure in his upbringing – and how much in his later life?

To my, and maybe your, surprise, the answer is a very great deal and in fact he rode more extensively than any British Prime Minister before or since. Maybe we shouldn't be surprised. Winston Churchill was born a full 20 years before the first car was driven on a British

WSC at Bangalore, 1896

highway, making spectators goggle and horses bolt. Both sides of his family had horses as a necessary part of their existence, as well as a major source of their pleasure. For Winston, horses were his escape in childhood, his challenge in youth, his transport in war, his triumph in sport and his diversion in dotage. They were even involved the day before he was born. The rough ride his mother had whilst returning in a pony trap from a shooting party caused Churchill's premature birth in an ante-room at Blenheim Palace in the early hours of 30 November 1874.

For this child of distant parents, trotting the pony Rob Roy around his grandfather the Duke of Marlborough's ancestral park at Blenheim was one of the solaces of an often lonely childhood. As the little accident-prone boy grew to frail-framed adulthood, riding horses increasingly became the means of proving the courage that was to become the very core of his being. Physical and mental courage are not always shared in the same person. I am here to tell you that pulling the goggles down and galloping at the first fence in a steeplechase can at times seem far less daunting than fronting up a big TV programme, let alone, as in Winston's case, taking on the leadership of a world whose very existence is under threat. For me, the central fascination of researching this book was to discover how fearless Churchill was in body as well as mind.

For while he struggled to even enter the Royal Military Academy at Sandhurst, three terms later he passed out in the top set of cadets and gained second place overall in the riding exam. Such equestrian attainment heightened into fox hunting, point-to-pointing and steeplechasing, and an early obsession with polo, climaxing with a winning hat-trick in the coveted Inter-Regimental Cup Final at Meerut in India. His courage, and that trained suppleness in the saddle which saw him survive the dramas of the charge at Omdurman, again saved his life two years later in South Africa during the Boer War, by enabling him to grab a stirrup and vault up behind his mounted rescuer after a seemingly fatal ambush.

It also meant that when Winston had already achieved high political status, he had the expertise as well as the enthusiasm to undertake an arduous and highly hazardous horseback safari in Kenya in 1907, lead a 1,200-horse gallop at Yeomanry camp in 1911, go boar hunting in France, continue playing polo into his fifties and, in November 1948, just three days shy of his 74th birthday, hire a horse and hack off with the Old Surrey and Burstow Hunt in protest against an upcoming bill against fox hunting.

Even riding was not enough. In 1949, at the ripe old age of 74, Churchill bought a three-year-old from France called Colonist II which, as a gallant, front-running grey, went on to win 13 races and trigger 13 extraordinary, ecstatic scenes as his Homburg-hatted, cigar-chewing owner gave 'V for Victory' signs in the unsaddling enclosure. Many other winners followed, mostly bred by Churchill himself.

I doubt if any of this influenced the millions who voted Winston Churchill the 'Greatest Briton in History' in the 2002 BBC poll. But, almost 150 years since that fateful baby first blinked at the Oxfordshire dawn, it's easy to forget how familiar the jingle of harness, clop of hoof and snorting of nostril were to the ordinary music of his day.

Over the years I have galloped horses in five different continents. I have played polo, hunted where Winston hunted, raced where he raced and, for an earlier book, trekked where he trekked under the South African sun. For this book I have been to the Sudan to ride the trail to Omdurman, and to Cuba to canter where he celebrated, if that is the word, his 21st birthday by being shot at by Cuban rebels whilst on horseback with the Spanish forces. For security reasons I have given the Swat Valley a miss, but have been given intriguing if deliberately incomplete information by my younger son, who experienced several dramas beyond even Churchill's whilst out there with the Special Forces in Afghanistan.

Wherever possible I have tried to lead with pictures. A long journalistic career working alongside some great photographers soon disabused me of the idea that anyone would read my first line before they looked at a compelling picture.

But there is one picture I have missed. It is of Winston Churchill riding the famous warhorse Warrior, who spent five years with my grandfather Jack Seely in France, and returned to win a race, the Isle of Wight point-to-point in 1922. In researching my book *Galloper Jack* I found that all sorts of people, like Sir John French and F.E. Smith, rode Warrior in France. F.E., the greatest barrister of his era, Lord Chancellor in the post-war Cabinet (as Lord Birkenhead) and Churchill's closest friend, came down to stay with Grandpa on the Isle of Wight and rode Warrior out hunting. Winston and my grandfather were also great friends, having served in the Asquith government together. There are family records of the great man coming to visit, and my mother used to relate a memory of this small but dominating young man marching her and her many siblings down to the beach to build the most complicated of sandcastles. But photos of Winston riding Warrior there are none. It looks like a job for Photoshop.

He would certainly have been up for it. After all, one of the most quoted of Churchill's sayings is his encouragement of young people to ride horses: 'The worst that can happen is that they break their necks. And that, at the gallop, is a very good death to die.'

This is not a proper history book: I have nothing but respect and awe for the amazing works over which I have pored, the historians I have consulted, and the endless letters and anecdotes that have been so comprehensively compiled by the unique source that is the Churchill Archives Centre in Cambridge. All I offer is an attempt to go back in time and look at Churchill from the only vantage point where I can claim any authority: a view from the saddle. **BS**

WSC greets Colonist in the unsaddling
enclosure at Hurst Park

01

EARLY MEMORIES: EMO PARK, 1879

"My picture of her in Ireland is in a riding habit, fitting like a skin and often beautifully spotted with mud. She and my father hunted continually on their large horses; and sometimes there were great scares because one or the other did not get back for many hours after they were expected."

Donkeys are not easy rides at the best of times. They may look sweet, but so do zebras, and you get on one of those at your peril. The neck is so short, and the head so big, that steering tends to be by the donkey's consent rather than your choosing. Trust me, it can be hard enough for an adult. Back in the summer of 1879 it was certainly too much for the four-year-old Winston Churchill, when his nurse took alarm and the donkey shied in the stately grounds of Emo Park in County Laois, 50 miles south-west of Dublin, the home of his late Aunt Aline's widower, the Earl of Portarlington.

The recollections are understandably hazy, since they depend on Churchill's book *My Early Life*, written in 1929. By this account he ended up unconscious after being catapulted from the donkey's saddle. The extraordinary circumstances of why he was there and what his family were doing may be hard to believe, but not impossible to imagine, and are important as an equestrian snapshot of the era.

These days Emo Court stands exactly as classically proud as it would have done when the child Winston was taken there all those years ago. From the great columned porch, the windowed wings and the grand green rotunda you look out down the longest tree-flanked avenue of its type in Ireland. It was down there that Churchill thinks the soldiers were drilling, and it was at this that the donkey took fright.

Visit nowadays, and it will suddenly hit you how utterly dependent everyone back then would have been on four-legged transport. The railway line from Dublin to Portarlington may have been completed in 1854, but it would still have needed a carriage to travel the five miles on to Emo Park, and a horse, or in this case a donkey, to get you anywhere else. It will also hit you how astonishingly, and at times almost comically, privileged a background our little donkey rider enjoyed.

Winston was the grandson of the Duke of Marlborough, who in 1876 had reluctantly agreed to become Viceroy of Ireland, with Churchill's father Lord Randolph as his secretary, in order to remove the latter from the ire of Edward, Prince of Wales. The old Duke's reluctance was understandable: his annual income from the Blenheim estates was £20,000 (a handy £2 million in 2017), while the cost of being Viceroy was £40,000 – equivalent to a whopping £4 million back then.

The Prince's anger was equally easy to appreciate. Lord Randolph, in taking his wayward brother Lord Blandford's side in a messy divorce case, had gained possession of compromising letters from the future monarch to the lady in question. Taking them to the Princess of Wales was little short of blackmail, and he compounded the offence by swaggering around London crowing, 'I have the crown of England in my pocket.' Bertie was so furious that he challenged Randolph to a duel with pistols in the south of France.

While none of this aristocratic huffing and puffing would have had any meaning to the four-year-old boy about to be pitched off the donkey, moving to Ireland certainly did. For his father it was a political awakening that kick-started his doomed but meteoric career, the emulation of which would so inspire Winston's later life, and the Irish location meant that his first impressions of his parents would often be of them in hunting mode.

Lord Randolph had been deeply involved with hunting from an early age, and even ran his own pack of hounds, the Blenheim Harriers, whilst a student at Oxford. But it's hard not to believe that for Winston it was his mother in the saddle who made the deepest impact. 'My picture of her in Ireland,' Winston wrote of his stunningly attractive mother, 'is in a riding habit, fitting like a skin and often beautifully spotted with mud. She and my father hunted continually on their large horses; and sometimes there were great scares because one or the other did not get back for many hours after they were expected.' She was, as in so many things, very good at it.

In 1879 Jennie Churchill may have been only 24, but she was already an accomplished, as well as a titled and extremely striking, young lady. 'She had a forehead like a panther's and great wild eyes that looked through you,' wrote the future Prime Minister's wife Margot Asquith on first meeting. 'She was so arresting that I followed her about till I found someone who could tell me who she was.' Jennie

Jennie Churchill and Randolph Churchill

Mrs Elizabeth Everest, WSC's beloved nanny and confidante

had spent three years in Paris, as well as her childhood in New York. She was a good singer, a fine linguist, a talented artist and a pianist skilled enough to later play duets with Paderewski. But in Ireland it was what she could do with the reins in her hands that worked the magic.

All this was in her genes. Her father, Leonard Jerome, maker and loser of several Manhattan fortunes, was famed as the first man to drive a coach four-in-hand up the streets of New York, as well as being the founding father of the New York Jockey Club and the creator of New York's first racecourse at the inevitably named Jerome Park. He also had a penchant for sugar-daddying sopranos, and a watchword that the two greatest sins for a young woman were 'to sing a false note or to jerk a good horse in the mouth'. Jennie did neither.

Indeed, one of the sugar-daddied sopranos reported that the Jerome daughters 'rode like Amazons', and both Jennie's letters and contemporary reports only confirm the splendid passage in her own, admittedly sometimes quite unreliable, memoirs that in Ireland

hunting became our ruling passion. Whenever I could 'beg, borrow or steal' a horse I did so. We had a few horses of our own which we rode indiscriminately and, both of us being light-weights, many were 'the tosses' I took, as the Irish papers used to call them. But it was glorious sport, and to my mind even hunting in Leicestershire could not compare with it.

Reading the reports now would dazzle a society columnist, let alone a four-year-old from the nursery.

In modern-day Britain, hunting is usually pictured as a peripheral as well as controversial activity. How great the contrast with the late 19th century, when it was seen as the most sought-after of pursuits. This was certainly the case in Ireland. In 1878 the Viceroy, as well as Jennie and Randolph, were recorded as staying at Knockdrin Castle to hunt with the West Meath; the next season the fields of the county were also adorned by Ireland's most famous hunting visitor, Elisabeth, Empress of Austria, wife of Franz Joseph, the assassination of whose nephew Franz Ferdinand triggered the First World War.

Elisabeth was a truly fascinating little figure. She was minuscule, under eight stone, with a 19-inch waist and an early health food obsession, and yet able to handle any horse, despite usually riding with an open fan in front of her face. She arrived with 12 hunters, and an entourage that included the impossibly gallant figure of George 'Bay' Middleton as Master of the Horse. Bay, who would eventually be killed in a race in Warwickshire in April 1892, could be as charming out of the saddle as in it, and his 18-month affair with Lady Blanche Hozier led many to believe, including Lady Blanche herself, that he was the father of her daughter Clementine, who in 1908 would become the wife of one Winston Spencer Churchill.

The banks and ditches of County Meath are not for the faint-hearted. When I went out with the Ward Union Staghounds, the Irish champion jockey Paul Carberry disappeared into one watery trap, only to come thundering past three fields later completely sodden, as though he and his horse had been through a particularly muddy car wash. It was unlikely to have been any easier back in the 1870s – and don't forget that Jennie and the Empress were doing all this riding side-saddle.

The papers were star-struck by their Austrian visitor, and the *Irish Times* reported 500 followers and a 'Welcome to the Empress' placard for the St Patrick's Day meet at Culmullen, but ultimately the circumstances that led to little Winston falling off his donkey had darker and deeper roots.

This was the terrible era of the potato famine. Potatoes were the principal component of the peasantry's diet, and so the blight that caused persistent failure of the crop resulted in mass starvation, and in turn mass emigration. The Great Famine of 1845–52 had seen the population of Ireland fall from 8 to 6.5 million, and it continued to drop through the rest of the century. A horribly wet summer in 1879 brought another blight to the soggy potatoes, and Jennie writes of the pitiful conditions of the ragged peasantry she saw as she trotted by.

WSC aged five

It has been related many times how all this changed the course of Irish history, producing an Irish diaspora many times the size of the state itself (30% of the population of Boston by the end of the century), and permanently souring Anglo-Irish relations. The old Duke of Marlborough had been Lord President of the Council in Disraeli's Tory government, and in 1873, mostly as a sop to get his father's consent to the Jerome marriage, the young Randolph Churchill had been elected MP for the family seat in Woodstock. His parliamentary contributions had at first been fairly minimal, but now suddenly, instead of being swept up in the intrigue and corridor-creeping of London and county society, in Ireland he was confronted with issues of the harshest kind. He did not give them an unsympathetic hearing.

He may still have been keen on his hunting, but he was much more intent on getting his voice heard on Irish affairs, and as early as September 1877 spoke out at Westminster, blaming successive British governments for neglect and siding with the Irish Nationalists in their parliamentary tactics of 'Obstructionism'. In Ireland itself he took on a much more practical role. His mother, to her credit, rallied round to raise over £100,000 in famine relief (£10 million in today's money), and during that year Randolph personally visited every Irish county, the dandyish, pop-eyed, over-moustachioed figure from Westminster transformed into an eager and well-informed hand on the rescue cart.

But no one should imagine that this would satisfy the aching anger of Irish patriots, any more than it did the gnawing hunger of the starving peasantry. You certainly won't if you visit Emo Park now. The drive, the walls and the gatehouse are all there today: what could the ordinary Irishman, let alone a starving peasant, have thought of the immaculately attired overseas 'swells' as their carriage swept inside the park walls and down the long empty drive, where grooms would lead the horses away and the visitors stroll down to the lake past those statues of Hellenic deity?

Winston's childhood memory is of a difficult relationship.

'It was borne in on me,' he writes in that engagingly cryptic tone with which he handled his childhood in *My Early Life*, 'that the Irish were a very ungrateful people; they did not say so much as "Thank you" for the entertainments, nor even for "The Famine Fund".' Much more dramatic, and more relevant to the disaster with the donkey, were the Fenians, who, in the eyes of many, in particular Winston's nanny Elizabeth Everest, figured high in local demonology: 'I gathered these were wicked people, and that there was no end to what they would do if they had their way.'

The Fenian Brotherhood had been founded in the USA, and in the 1860s had as many as 6,000 men under arms over there, and planned a number of raids against British possessions in Canada. In Ireland in 1879 they had not yet made a major impact. But they soon would. In July 1882, in the very grounds of the Vice-Regal Lodge where the young Winston would have tottered alongside Mrs Everest, two members of a Fenian offshoot stabbed and killed Lord Frederick Cavendish, the Chief Secretary for Ireland, and Thomas Burke, its most senior civil servant. Three years earlier Mr Burke had endeared himself to Winston by giving him a toy drum. The news from Dublin boomed out confirmation of all the Fenian fears Mrs Everest and many others had harboured, although Churchill later acknowledged in *My Early Life* that what the donkey was actually shying from that day at Emo Park was a standard route march of the local Rifle Brigade.

'I loved my mother dearly,' wrote Winston – 'but at a distance. My nurse was my confidante. Mrs Everest it was who looked after me and tended all my wants. It was to her that I poured out all my troubles.' Mrs Everest, his devoted 'Woomanly', was the sheet anchor of his early life whilst, as was the custom in aristocratic families at the time, the parents played an infinitely more hands-off role than that of today's nappy-changing multi-taskers. It was Mrs Everest, with of course the groom, who was beside Winston as the donkey walked up the path in Emo Park.

The four-year-old Winston was already a talkative little thing, and Mrs Everest was much more likely to be trying to hold him steady on his mount than sharing her fears of Fenians. Up ahead of them would be the famous long avenue of cedars, named Wellingtonias when planted in 1852 to mark the death of the Duke of Wellington, the hero of Waterloo, but originally a native of Dublin and County Meath, and in 1822 godfather to Lady Frances Vane, who was to become Winston's grandmother.

Emo Park, County Laois, where WSC fell
off the donkey

Somewhere amongst those trees would have come the sounds
and shouts of marching men. It may in reality have been the Rifle
Brigade on a route march – but you can imagine the startled horror
as the nanny jumped back and exclaimed, 'It's the Fenians!' You know
what the donkey would do. Little boys of four did not 'ride' in the real
sense: they just sat on a makeshift saddle. When the donkey shied,
they went head-first over the side. The rest, according to the boy's
own account, was silence.

As Winston passed into unconsciousness it was still 37 years
before Dublin's Easter Rising. Nowadays, 100 yards from the entrance
to Emo Park stands a dignified memorial to commemorate its cente-
nary. Emo Court may not look that different, but a lot of things have
changed, most of them for the better. In later life Churchill was to be
much occupied with Irish affairs, first opposing Home Rule before
espousing it as part of the Liberal government, and then being a major
player in the game-changing Anglo-Irish Treaty of 1921.

But back in England the first aim would be to stay in the saddle.

02

BLENHEIM AND BEYOND: HOVE, 1880–1890

"I rode Robroy round the park today and rode him all by myself in the school."

Previous page: WSC, the schoolboy; *above:* WSC, the steady gaze

Rob Roy was not always the perfect pony, but he does have his place in history. He was the first animal to be written about by Winston Churchill.

The letter, to his mother in April 1882, is as touching as its address is magnificent. It is sent from Blenheim Palace which, with its Vanbrugh design and Capability Brown landscape, makes Emo Court look little more than a modest manor house. The seven-year-old Winston and his two-year-old brother Jack were staying at Blenheim with the old Duke and Duchess as his mother helped his father recover from a serious health scare that had incapacitated him in February. Winston's may, in many ways, have been a life of ultimate privilege, but the letter is still one from a little boy who misses his parents and is already exceptionally descriptive with the pen – if not yet completely comfortable in the saddle.

> *Blenheim*
> *My Dear Mamma,*
>
> *I got your letter today & am so glad to hear that Papa is better. Grandmama has just come. I have been out riding Rob Roy today in the Park he was very fresh so Chapman had to ride him first 20 times round the school and led me in the park. There are a great many violets in the gardens. Jack does like gathering the daises so much. We went down to see Grandpapa at breakfast this morning.*
>
> *With many kisses and love from*
> *Winston.*

In less than a hundred words we have the most vivid of images. In his own book Winston may portray his parents as remote and, particularly in his father's case, comparatively uncaring. But both the quantity and quality of the letters exchanged between Winston and his parents, and indeed between Jennie and Randolph, tell a rather different story.

In these days of dumbed-down texts and 140-character tweets it is instructive to see how often and how much Winston's family communicated by letter. Jennie and Randolph may have had the Victorian upper-class versions of the 'open marriage', but they were constantly keeping each other in touch with their children, their social life, Randolph's politics and their horses. 'Rode the chestnut in a martingale this time and she carried her head perfectly', runs a letter of Jennie's from Ireland – the talk of one rider to another.

Winston may have described his mother as a 'distant star' but, while he would never have read the diary she kept in the early months of 1882, he would have been neither unaware of nor unimpressed by at least two of the main pursuits recorded in its pages. For example:

Blenheim Park

in the seven days of 8 to 14 January, Jennie hunted with the Quorn on Saturday and Monday from Sysonby Lodge, the 'hunting box' the Churchills used to take at Melton Mowbray; with the Fitzwilliam on the Wednesday from Burghley House, home of the Marquis of Exeter; and then back to Melton to go out with the Cottesmore on the Saturday. The following week in London she painted every day. From this we can see where Winston got his energy, and also understand how and why painting came to be a saving grace in later life. But we also need to acknowledge just how important were the horses.

Yet the riding Winston's first letter depicts is very much of the novice kind, and anyone who has ever tried to get their child started in the saddle will understand the early mismatch of the feather-light infant and the frisky pony. Too often the parent or keeper fails to prevent scary moments, and a consequent permanent dislike of the riding experience. 'Chapman' the groom would have been one of an extensive Blenheim stable staff having to service everything from the ducal carriage to the pony trap. When Rob Roy lurched and Winston flinched, the loyal retainer would have known what to do. These ponies were descended from animals who worked 12 hours a day as beasts of burden: 'Twenty times round the school' would be a minimum to get the little terror's back down and make him an amenable mount for Master Winston on the leading rein.

But what a location Blenheim would have been. What was then the stable block now houses a Churchill museum, but if you saddle up today and trot off round the park, it's not difficult to think of Chapman with our future hero on the leading rein. Perhaps they went out through the beech wood and then down into the dingle, and up the other side of the lake to where the monument to Winston's great-great-great-great-great grandfather reaches so starkly towards the sky. Back then an avenue of elm trees led up from the bridge, but disease took them in the 1970s, and hopeful young alders grow prettily in their place. In April the violets still bloom, and would no doubt have sat easier on the little boy's descriptive eye than the extraordinarily dense wodges of adulatory text which still cover all four sides of the first Duke's memorial.

One hundred and thirty-five years on we have only a few pieces with which to try and assemble the jigsaw of memory, but a month after this first letter there is another to 'My dear Mama'. It has the same clear and rounded lettering traced along the double-lined spacing, the same longing for her to come – 'Jack and I both want you very much' – but it also has a new-found sense of pride. 'I rode Robroy [*sic*] round the park today and rode him all by myself in the school.' Ah, 'all by myself'! – I hear the echo of my own son saying the very same thing three decades ago.

No doubt such idyllic outings continued on later visits to Blenheim, but it is noticeable that there are few other references to riding until after November 1884, when Winston was moved from his first boarding school at St George's, Ascot, an unhappy experience, to a smaller and much kinder academy in Hove. This was run by the Misses Thompson at the top of what was then the very elegant Brunswick Road, running 500 yards to the promenade and the Channel shore a mile west of Brighton's West Pier. Reading not just Churchill's but other pupils' accounts of the regime during his time at St George's it is not surprising that riding isn't mentioned. The bloody bare-bottom beatings, in one disgusting instance inducing the poor individual to soil himself, inflicted by the sadistic Reverend Herbert William Sneyd-Kynnersley, would have ruled out sitting in the saddle for weeks.

Jennie Churchill with her two boys.
Jack (left) and Winston (right)

But once Winston was at school in Hove his letters from there show that at this time in his young life riding was a pleasure, not an obsession. He was not one of those children for whom the pony and its stable becomes the centre of the universe, and from what one can judge, he was not that precocious in his achievements. For when, in January 1885, he writes to his mother, 'I have been out riding today and rode without the leading rein and we cantered,' it suggests that up to then being on the leading rein had been the norm. As a ten-year-old I was far from being the star of the Pony Club, but I would have thought it pretty sissy to still be on the leading rein.

Winston's wonderfully diverse letters from Brunswick Road about his many school activities speak of cricket, football, swimming, dancing, poetry and even a brief passion for the cello. But riding must have ranked pretty high, for just four days after that first letter he lists a routine: 'I ride three times a week. I have one hour on Tuesday, an hour and a half on Wednesday and an hour on Friday.' That's quite a commitment for a ten-year-old. Subsequent letters ask for a 'nice riding suit as my trousers always come up to my knees which look anything but pretty' and, touchingly in the summer of 1885, 'Do please let me go on with my riding as I am getting on so nicely. I enjoy it more than anything else.'

The attempt to follow what we might term Churchill's hoofprints can be as frustrating as it is evocative. For while what was the Misses Thompsons' whitewashed four-storey establishment at the top of Brunswick Road remains a fine, if rather faded, example of Brighton's terraced Victorian heyday, it has not been able to hang on to its surroundings like Emo Park and Blenheim. Just a quarter of a mile down the hill, the promenade and the sea still beckon, but the ageing, balconied elegance of the houses has been forced to incorporate such attractions as both a Chinese and an Indian takeaway, flanked by a tanning salon and a disc jockey's booking office. And while back in 1885 the crest of Brunswick Road would have been on the very edge of the countryside, the Misses Thompsons' school is now a YMCA hostel called Lansworth House and has townscape above it almost all the way up to the busy dual carriageway that is the A27.

All the more reason why one should try and imagine our already high-spirited little hero, 'the naughtiest small boy in the world' according to his dancing mistress, setting off on one of his thrice-weekly riding sessions. With the motor car still a decade away, many stables would be close at hand, and it's safe to assume that Winston would have cantered up the side of what was then called Chalybeate, but is now St Ann's Well Gardens, complete with cafe, playground, tennis courts, croquet lawn, bird guide and even a very modern Brighton 'LGBT Tree'.

Traffic lengthens every journey nowadays, but it is a trip of only a couple of miles east, across the top of the town, to arrive on Whitehawk Hill, from where the racecourse looks out to sea just as it

Riding in the park, WSC's first known letter to his mother

Happiness can be hacking on a pony

would have done in Churchill's time, 60 years before Graham Greene gave the track immortality in *Brighton Rock*. Imagine that the young Winston had hacked across from Hove: he would have found an aura about the place. For at the end of the 18th century the course had been patronised by the Prince Regent, and 50 years later the coming of the railway made it fashionable again, with the Brighton Cup becoming one of the great races of the season.

Back in the 1880s the racetrack would have been clear of the town, and while today assorted, rather grubby housing estates creep like ivy up the side of the valley, the steep climb and cambers of the racecourse still beckon. I remember only a few years back riding out for the then local trainer Gary Moore, and winging up towards the skyline with the spirit soaring as the hooves sang. For any rider, especially 'the naughtiest small boy in the world', a sweeping gallop up the springy turf of the Sussex Downs is as irresistible an invitation as the crisp snow on an open slope in Switzerland. Boys of all ages should not be denied their racing dreams once in the saddle, especially not if they will later need to gallop to save their skin.

The little figure going out from Brunswick Road in his riding kit was sometimes quite a frail one. Winston's health, and particularly his chest, had long caused general concern, so there had been other reasons beside the beatings for the move from St George's, Ascot. What Hove offered was the twin bonus of sea air and the home of the distinguished Dr Robson Roose, whose son Robert was also at the Misses Thompsons, and who in March 1886 nursed the young Winston back from what looked to be a fatal bout of double pneumonia.

Much has been made, mostly from Winston's own account in *My Early Life*, of his distant relationship with his father. But, as has been quite brilliantly argued by Celia and John Lee in their book *Winston and Jack*, an allowance for the customs of the time and a re-reading of the letters paint a very different picture. What is certain is that Churchill hero-worshipped his father, as is demonstrated in a letter from Brunswick Road at this time.

> *My darling Papa,*
>
> *I hope you are quite well. The weather continues fine although there has been a little rain lately. I have been out riding with a gentleman who thinks that Gladstone is a brute and thinks that 'the one with the curly moustache ought to be Premier'. The driver of the Electric Railway said 'that Lord R. Churchill would be Prime Minister'. Cricket has become the foremost thought now. Everybody wants your autograph but I can say I can only try, and I should like you to sign your name in full at the end of your letter. I only want a scribble as I know that you are very busy indeed.*

With love and kisses.
I remain your loving son.
Winston.

As you can guess from the letter, at that time Randolph was very much the shooting star of British politics. From 1880 to 1886 he rose from being a thorn in his own Conservative Party's side and a firecracker opponent of the Liberal government, to being Secretary of State for India, then Chancellor of the Exchequer and Leader of the House of Commons, before his impulsive and politically fatal resignation in December 1886, when his proposed cuts in military expenditure failed to find backing. He was still only 37.

To gather quite what an impact Lord Randolph made on the general public, let alone on his impressionable elder son, it is worth quoting his Oxford friend but political opponent Lord Rosebery, an Olympian figure but, like so many people in this story, quite a card, too, who is supposed to have struck a bet that he could land the treble of winning the Derby, becoming Prime Minister and marrying the richest woman in England, and actually pulled it off in reverse order: marrying Hannah, heiress to the Rothschild millions, in 1878; becoming Prime Minister in March 1894; and winning the Derby, for the first of three times, with Ladas three months later. Lord Rosebery said of Lord Randolph:

> *He was brilliant, courageous, resourceful, and unembarrassed*
> *by scruple: he had fascination, audacity, tact; great and solid*
> *ability welded with the precious gift of concentration; mar-*
> *vellous readiness in debate, and an almost unrivalled skill and*
> *attraction on the platform; for he united in an eminent degree*
> *both the Parliamentary and the popular gifts, a combination*
> *which is rarer than usually supposed.*

No wonder the other boys wanted Winston to get his autograph. It was to the turf that Lord Rosebery's Oxford friend Randolph turned when he so foolishly blew his political career, and over the next few years there would be much more to hero-worship here for his ginger-haired son and heir. Childhood pony trips at Blenheim and Brighton were one thing; riding out with the racehorses on Newmarket Heath watching your father's Classic winner quite another.

Lord Randolph at Newmarket

count Charles Kinsky.

H.C. Banks Lith

03

NEWMARKET AND OTHER EDUCATION, 1890

"Here I am at Banstead leading what
to me is an ideal existence."

Previous page: Count Charles Kinsky, heroic figure for WSC; *above*: Banstead Manor, near Newmarket, the happiest of homes for WSC

Banstead Manor, four miles south-east of Newmarket in Suffolk, is today renowned across the racing world as the centre of Prince Khalid Abdullah's racing empire, and as such the home of Frankel, Britain's most famous living racehorse and now most sought-after stallion. It has another claim to fame. It is where the young Winston had some of the best times of his life, both in and out of the saddle.

The ride up from there through Cheveley, then along the Ashtead Road back towards Newmarket, before hacking across the open turf to watch the horses working on Warren Hill, and then over the Bury Road onto the legendary 'Limekilns' gallop, is one to lift the heart. Think of the thrill it must have given Churchill when he did it for the first time with his father in the summer of 1890. Banstead Manor had become the house of dreams.

For Lord Randolph's dabble with the turf had become so successful that he had rented a base near the centre of the Suffolk town 15 miles east of Cambridge that, from its beginnings under Charles II, had become the very heartbeat of the horseracing game. In 1890 Newmarket boasted two racecourses, many surrounding stud farms, a thousand horses in training, and the home of the ruling Jockey Club, of which Lord Randolph would soon become a member.

Horseracing itself, moreover, was then the most prestigious of all sporting pursuits, and Derby Day the number one date in the sporting calendar. In 1888 the thoroughbred racehorse was also the Formula 1 car of sport, the fastest a young man could travel unless he jumped off a cliff en route to eternity. The most coveted of prizes were the five 'Classics', which tested the speed, courage and endurance of the three-year-old 'Classic' generation. The 2,000 Guineas for colts and the 1,000 Guineas for fillies were run over a straight mile at Newmarket at the beginning of May. The Derby for colts and the Oaks for fillies took place over a left-handed, mile-and-a-half, steeply undulating, horseshoe-shaped helter-skelter of a track on Epsom Downs at the beginning of June. And finally the St Leger, at Town Moor, Doncaster, was for both colts and fillies, over a sweeping, left-handed mile and three-quarters with a full four-furlong final straight, and was run at the start of September each year.

Crowned heads all over Europe and beyond were taking a leaf out of Leonard Jerome's book and creating racecourses of their own, using the English thoroughbred as their stock and usually English staff to tend them. Horseracing was very much one of the jewels of the British Empire, which Churchill was born to worship, and would later, as a soldier and finally war leader, pledge his heart to defend. When the champion jockey Fred Archer tragically committed suicide in 1886 there was national mourning: at Newmarket his funeral cortege stretched right round the town and was headed by a personal representative of the Prince of Wales.

At the Doncaster Sales in 1887 Lord Randolph and his friend Lord Dunraven bought a yearling which had been raised by a John Snarry on Musley Bank near Malton – nowadays, as racing experts will know, the base of the record-breaking trainer Richard Fahey. The yearling was a small, almost black filly, by a sire called Trappist, out of a mare called Festive, and sent to be trained by Bob Sherwood at Newmarket. There was much talk at the time of a scandalous new French novel in which a beautiful young abbess breaks her vow of chastity on the eve of what she thinks is to be both her and her lover's execution – only to find in the morning that she is spared – and at Jennie Churchill's saucy suggestion the filly was named after the book: L'Abbesse De Jouarre. Punters soon revised this to 'Abscess on the Jaw', but to Lady Randolph the horse was 'a gallant little thing with a heart bigger than her body'.

Winston, meanwhile, often sick and seemingly unfocused, had been giving Jennie and Randolph plenty of heartache. There had been an ugly moment at Hove when Miss Thompson had reported that Winston stabbed another boy in the hand with a knife. In April 1888 he was sent to public school – not, like his father, to Eton, but to Harrow, that other great educator of the Victorian mighty, whose position high on the hill north of London was thought better for Churchill's health. The school's punishment book records a 'flogging' for breaking into a local shed, and his younger cousin Shane Leslie (son of Jennie's sister Leonie) remembers him as the 'enfant terrible of a home circle, a fearless, sandy-haired youth, untidy, unmanageable and quick of speech'.

Yet while Winston's inability to handle maths and Latin kept him in the lower forms at Harrow, and aimed him for Sandhurst and the Army rather than university and the Bar, he was brilliant enough to win a declamation prize in his first term by faultlessly reciting 1,200 lines of Macaulay, bold enough to write Establishment-knocking letters under a pseudonym to the *Harrovian*, and resource-ful enough to dictate class-topping English essays to a senior boy in exchange for help with his own Latin translation. He was also devoted enough, even in that immensely snobby environment, to greet the plump, nanny figure of Mrs Everest at Harrow station and march arm-in-arm with her up the high street. 'It was the bravest thing I ever saw,' said a fellow pupil.

Lord Randolph's Oaks winner L'Abbesse De Jouarre with her foal

Even now at such establishments, the kudos an association with horseracing success would give a boy among his peers would be sub-stantial. So imagine what it did for the street cred of young Winston at a time when racing was so glamorous, followed by all strands of society, and everyone liked a winner, when L'Abbesse won four races as a two-year-old in her first season and then, first time out in 1889, won the Oaks at a whopping 20-1!

We know what happened after she won the Manchester Cup in May of the next season at the same odds, because Winston wrote to his parents.

Heath House, Newmarket in 1884 by
A.L. Townshend featuring champion
St Simon in the foreground, trainer
Matt Dawson mounted in the top hat,
and jockey Fred Archer, also mounted,
alongside

To Lord Randolph:
My dear Papa

*I have been congratulated on all quarters on account of the
'fluky filly'. When I went to telegraph at the post office, the man
who took my telegram informed me that he had 'dropped a quid
hover* [sic] *that there 'orse'. I drank the Abbess's health in lemon
squash and we eat her luck in strawberry rash.*

And even better to 'My Darling Mamma': 'Good old "Habbess".
I got a full account from Jack of the race and of the Duke of
Cambridge's nose, not flattering to his Royal and Military Highness.'
 Altogether, in her four seasons on the track, L'Abbesse won eight
races, including the Hardwicke Stakes as a five-year-old at Royal
Ascot in 1891.
 'I am so glad you are going to take that place near Newmarket,'
Winston wrote to his father in June 1890. For a family of profi-
cient riders it was from the start, as Jennie wrote in her memoir,
an idyllic retreat:

> *We often rode out in the early morning from six to seven to see
> the horses on the gallops. It was a healthy and invigorating life,
> and I became greatly interested, spending hours with Randolph
> at Sherwood's, when he and the trainer would study the racing
> calendar and decide upon the entries for the horses.*

 Two months after his letter Winston, Jack, Mrs Everest and
Missey the dog trotted up in the carriage from Newmarket station
to spend a much-anticipated holiday themselves at Banstead. Lord
Randolph was to join them at the end of the week, but Jennie had
taken her mother away to France for a break. It was to 'Grand Hotel,

Aix-les-Bains, Savoie', therefore, that Winston wrote one of his most charming letters. In it, as he relates how they await the arrival of Lord Randolph before they can go shooting, the energy, organisation and amusingly desperate filial affection leap from the page:

> *Riding at 8 and Ratting at 10.30 so I hope to enjoy myself tomorrow. We are going to arrange about a quiet pony for Jack and about getting up a Cricket Eleven and challenging the Village. Missey has been tremendously 'keen' lately but she had a small fit this evening. However she recovered allright and is v. lively.*
>
> *Jack sends you 14 pints of Love & 26 Brace of Kisses.*
>
> *With love from Winny,*
> *I remain*
> *Your loving Son*
> *Winston S. Churchill*

Meanwhile, Lord Randolph was staying at Brighton for the 'Sussex Fortnight', and writing daily bulletins to Jennie on his prowess, not all of it successful. L'Abbesse De Jouarre got beaten in the Brighton Cup, 'Tom Cannon got off badly and I have lost my money,' he writes grumpily on 31 July but, en route to join the boys at Newmarket, then claims he has 'cleared about £1,100 quid for the fortnight'. Men lie to their wives about many things, especially betting, but if this is in any way true it is spectacular money – £100,000 at today's rates.

Lord Randolph could be a difficult parent even before the final brain tumour which, rather than syphilis, is now argued as the more likely cause of his early death in 1895, began to eat into his personality. 'Your father is very angry with you,' Lady Randolph wrote to Winston after her son had failed to instantly thank his dad for a present sent after L'Abbesse De Jouarre's triumph in the Manchester Cup, 'for not acknowledging the gift of £5 for a whole week and then writing an offhand careless letter'. But by the time the filly's owner arrived at Banstead those £1,100 winnings would have put him in high good humour, and his son's hero-worship, rarely reciprocated, reached its apogee.

'Rode over to the Limekilns to watch the horses,' Lord Randolph wrote to Jennie that night. 'Winston rode the new pony. He rides well.' We can picture the pair: the 41-year-old father with his trademark moustache curling beneath the black top hat, the slight 15-year-old boy trotting beside him on his pony. Lord Randolph may have been out of office and searching for a role in life, but he was still the most charismatic politician in the land, and his presence would have spread swiftly over the Newmarket bush telegraph.

Today there are some 60 trainers and 2,000 horses in training in Newmarket, more than double the number during Lord Randolph's time, but back then there were only 4,000 people, compared to 20,000-plus today. In 1890, a quarter of Newmarket's population had four legs, not two! And while horseracing remains the most high-profile of all the town's activities, it is now a much more demarcated, parallel world, to allow the other 20,000 inhabitants of the town to carry on with lives completely unconnected to the horse. It's not always the easiest co-existence, as the horse does not rule as it would have done back in the days when the motor car was still unknown.

Riding was so much freer then. In October 1889 my Cambridge undergraduate grandfather and his friend Victor Cavendish, the future Duke of Devonshire, rode over to Newmarket from Trinity College, Cambridge to watch the Cambridgeshire, and were able to gallop beside the course ahead of the race until the field swept by. What's more, the two undergrads somehow backed the winner Laureate at 66-1, and rode back to Cambridge with their clothes stuffed with fivers.

But the addictive thrill of following a racehorse in its preparation remains. For six wonderful months in 2005 I rode out regularly from Michael Bell's Fitzroy House yard to chart the progress of Motivator, the favourite for and subsequent brilliant winner of that summer's Derby. Each morning we would thread our way out onto the horse walk on Rowley Drive, then past St Mary's Church to cross onto the open grass of the Severals, before waiting to stop understandably impatient car drivers on the main road in from Bury St Edmunds as they hurried schoolchildren and others towards the clock tower and into town.

Once onto the Heath proper we would normally then file across the much more minor route to Moulton, before spinning up Warren Hill, either on the grass strip allocated for that morning or up the railed all-weather track that runs beside it. On other days we would walk left along the Bury Road past Bedford Lodge, Stanley House and Clarehaven from where, respectively Luca Cumani, Godolphin and John Gosden have sent out Derby winners. This path would allow the main string to spin back along the artificial Al Bahathri gallop, or the selected few to go on further, and finally come back over the Limekilns. The turf here is so uniquely springy that horses are only allowed to work on it when the other grass gallops have got too hard, and it's over this whispering ancient grassland that all the great horses have been tested down the years.

The magic of riding and watching a racehorse is to sense the power that surges within. One moment the horse is walking sedately forward; the next it has sprung off and clicked into a zinging onward gallop with the wind tugging at its mane. As the horses stream along you imagine them in greater arenas, the crowd buzzing, the harlequin patterns of the jockeys' silks flashing by in the frenzy of a finish. Even today, out on the gallops of a Newmarket morning, the racehorse is still king. When Winston rode across with his father in 1890 it would have seemed that for the thoroughbred this was a domain over which the sun, as with the British Empire, would never set.

Special horse walks were no more needed then than railed-off gallops. The trainers' strings would file up the High Street or, in the case of Lord Randolph's trainer Bob Sherwood, up the Vicarage Road onto the gallops. At the foot of Warren Hill stood Heath House, where Sir Mark Prescott still skilfully tends the training flame, and from where in 1890 Fred Archer's old mentor Matt Dawson had already sent out three Derby winners, and his nephew George another two in 1888 and 1889. Such things are still mentioned now as you ride by: they would have buzzed in the ears of Winston Churchill. Was it not at Heath House that Matt Dawson had recently trained the legendary St Simon, never beaten or even extended in his nine races between 1883 and 1884, and already in his first season described by his trainer as 'certainly the best two-year-old I have ever trained – he will probably make the best racehorse that has ever run on the Turf'? They speak of him still.

Winston and his brother certainly did, because so many of their schoolfriends' relatives were heavily involved in racing too. Lady Randolph's close friend Laura, Countess of Wilton, for example, so supportive of Winston that she used to sign her letters to him 'Your Deputy Mother', would marry Sir Frederick Johnstone, who in 1891 won both the 2,000 Guineas and the Derby with a colt called Common who went on to win the St Leger and so land the coveted Triple Crown.

Count Charles Kinsky (middle) jumps the water on the way to winning the 1883 Grand National on Zoedone

A week after the Derby, Sir Frederick sent a letter to Winston at Harrow containing a £5 note and the hope that 'you will come down... this summer' to their place in Windsor. Think of the thrill that must have given to the 15-year-old with the red hair, wild ideas and rapid, slightly stammering speech, and remember that in today's money £5 was close to £500! At that time Winston Churchill had many good reasons to be interested in racing.

But there were many, many other things at Banstead with which Winston and Jack filled their days. They shot rabbits and terriered rats, while Winston's natural compulsion to organise others bore its first fruit in the construction of 'the Den', the now famous hut made of mud and planks, with a straw floor and a surrounding moat. Starting at Blenheim and on through Randolph Churchill's ever-changing abodes, Winston had built up a massive collection of toy soldiers, and fantasised about battle formations and cavalry charges. Now he could implement his defence and attack tactics by dragooning luckless cousins like little Shane Leslie.

By the age of 15, Churchill had already been to three boarding schools, and lived at Blenheim, Phoenix Park in Dublin, St James's Place and Connaught Place. 'Here I am at Banstead leading what to me is an ideal existence,' he wrote to his father. 'It is not possible to overestimate the joy that these two seemingly privileged but in fact rootless children derived,' says Celia Sandys of Winston and Jack in the Newmarket years, with an author's understanding as well as a granddaughter's insight, 'from being able to run wild in a place of their own.'

Winston was not yet up to much gambling, at least with money. But what was clearly forming in his mind was the need to take risks and prove his courage in life. In his first year at Harrow he wrote a remarkable 1,800-word essay, illustrated with no fewer than six maps, fantasising about a Colonel Seymour battling against the Russian forces in the Ukraine. It is full of action: 'seeing my opportunity, I jumped on a stray horse and rode for my life. Thud! Thud! and the hooves of a Cossack's horse came nearer and nearer behind me'.

And even though there remains a hypochondriac tone to his letters of the time – toothache, measles, flu, concussion – the little redhead was getting stronger. He did well at shooting in the Harrow Army Class. He got into the winning House swimming team, and in the spring and summer of 1891, to his great credit, won both the Harrow and the Public Schools Fencing Championships. But with his background and his slender frame, the chances of glory, of the Empire-building valour lauded in the G.A. Henty and H. Rider Haggard adventures he so loved (he read *King Solomon's Mines* 10 times), were more likely to come on horseback than any other way. And, by happy coincidence, a 24-carat hero for a role model was on hand extremely close to home, in his father's friend and his mother's lover, Count Charles Kinsky.

Quite how late Victorian mores squared off these relationships is hard to fathom, but the Count was certainly an object of avuncular splendour to the young Winston. Officially titled Prince Karel Andreas Kinsky, 'Count Charles' was heir to large family estates in Bohemia, and first came to England as part of the hunting entourage of the aforementioned Empress Elisabeth. He returned three years later as an attaché at the Austro-Hungarian Embassy, and quickly proved as brilliant on horseback as he was on the dance floor. In even bolder echoes of Lord Randolph's winnings at Brighton, at just 24 the Count won £1,000 on a single bet on the 1882 Cambridgeshire, and spent £800 on a five-year-old mare called Zoedone, with another £200 to come if she won the Grand National. Six months later she and the Count duly did. In 1884 they went again, and finished fifth, but a year after that she collapsed on the second circuit at the fence before Becher's after almost certainly being doped beforehand. 'Swash' and 'buckle' might epitomise her rider.

The galloping diplomat became enough of a fixture in Jennie's life to catch mumps from the boy he wrote to as 'My Dear Old Winny', and in the summer of 1891 to inspire a letter from Winston to the then 11-year-old Jack which is nothing short of adulatory. 'I hear your pony is a regular beauty and the fastest on Newmarket Heath but I don't believe he will beat the Gem' (Winston's steed), it begins, before recounting, in 16 glowing pages, how the Count took him to the Crystal Palace to see a display of fire engines and fireworks in honour of the German Emperor. The Count could do no wrong: 'crushed the hand' of an unfortunate attendant who tried to prevent them mounting the roller-coaster, found a table for 'a tolerable dinner with lots of champagne which pleased your loving brother', and then rocketed home in his phaeton: 'Count K drives beautifully and we passed with our fast horses everything on the road.'

When Winston finally passed the exams and got into Sandhurst to train as an army officer, and after that into the cavalry, it was a picture of Count Kinsky and Zoedone winning the Grand National that he hung on the wall. But there would be tough times and hard riding ahead, and while Lady Randolph's favourite Austrian may have been Winston's physical hero, it was the ailing and intemperate Lord Randolph who did his son the best favour in showing how to move on.

Prince of Wales (centre) rides back from the races

04

SANDHURST AND SADDLE PLANS, 1894–1895

"Horses were the greatest of my pleasures at Sandhurst," it begins. "I and the group in which I moved spent all our money on hiring horses from the very excellent local livery stables. We ran up bills on the strength of future commissions. We organised point-to-points and even a steeplechase in the park of a friendly grandee, and bucketed gaily about the countryside. And here I say to parents, 'Don't give your son money. As far as you can afford it, give him horses.'"

Previous page: WSC (left), the young cadet;
above: Captain Charles Burt, fabled riding
master for the Household Cavalry

The walk to the riding lessons on those February mornings in 1894 was a pretty smart one. So it would be if your grandmother's address was 50 Grosvenor Square, and your destination was Knightsbridge Barracks, on the other side of Rotten Row.

The 19-year-old Officer Cadet Winston Churchill is likely to have felt quite pleased with himself as he strode west down Upper Grosvenor Street, to pass among the carriages on Park Lane and then walk across Hyde Park for his appointment with Captain Charles Henry Burt, the fabled chief riding master of the Household Cavalry, who was to meet an unhappy and unusual end in April 1904 when thrown from carriage to pavement after his horse bolted in Piccadilly. Ten years earlier, fortune was kinder to our young cadet. He had a job, a plan, a girl, and was currently the next in line to be the Duke of Marlborough. Exactly a year earlier Winston's prospects had looked decidedly different.

On leaving Harrow he had received the news that he had failed the Sandhurst entrance exam a second time in February 1893. Having gone to holiday at his aunt's home in Dorset he was lucky to live after a reckless jump from a high bridge knocked him unconscious for three days with a ruptured kidney and a probable, but undiagnosed until a much later X-ray, fractured thigh. His mother was close to despair, his father to wrath.

Recovery, of both health and parental relations, was slow and had its setbacks, most notably later in August when Winston and Jack narrowly escaped drowning whilst swimming in Lake Geneva. But whilst recuperating in London from the Dorset accident, Winston met the likes of Rosebery, Asquith, Chamberlain and Balfour across the dining room table and was invited to lunch at the House of Commons by Edward Carson, the brilliant Irish barrister and newly elected MP who, 20 years on, would champion Ulster as one of Churchill's chief opponents in the crisis over Irish Home Rule.

In the summer of 1893, at the third attempt, he finally passed into the Royal Military Academy at Sandhurst, 95th out of 389 candidates, but still four places short of the mark required for his father's desired aim of an infantry cadetship. Needless to say, this did not worry Winston, who was aiming for the cavalry anyway.

Lord Randolph's initial reaction to what he saw as his son's over-self-congratulatory letter is one of the harshest eight-page put-downs in the history of father-son correspondence. 'If you cannot prevent yourself leading the idle, useless, unprofitable life you have in your schooldays,' it ended, 'you will become a mere social wastrel, one of the hundreds of public school failures, and you will degenerate into a shabby, unhappy and futile existence.'

The incandescent anger expressed in Lord Randolph's 'social wastrel' letter had something a bit more mercenary about it than mere rebuke for what he called 'your tone of exultation over your inclusion in the Sandhurst list'. Costs for a cavalry subaltern were £200 a year

more than for the infantry, and Lord Randolph, no mean spender himself, would be expected to stump up for his ever-importunate son. 'I had already formed a definite opinion upon the relative merits of riding and walking,' Winston would airily reflect when reminiscing in his fifties, but you can see Lord Randolph's side: 'in the infantry one has to keep a man,' he pointed out, 'in the cavalry a man and a horse as well.' What's more, with Winston one horse would never be enough – what about the polo ponies, and the hunters too?

Sure enough, within a month of Winston starting at Sandhurst in the September, and much to his irritation, Lord Randolph had person-ally contacted the Duke of Cambridge, the commander-in-chief of the army, to arrange for his son's future commission to be switched to the infantry, ensuring a place for the future subaltern in the 60th Rifles.

After a physically struggling start at the Royal Military Academy in the autumn of 1893, Winston had a successful first term, and he spent the first part of the Christmas holidays at Blenheim, hitherto long off-limits owing to a fraternal feud between Lord Randolph and the eighth duke that had only been resolved by the latter's death in November 1892. This now enabled Winston to form a deep and lifelong friendship with his three-years-older cousin Charles, by then the 8th Duke, but universally known to family and friends as 'Sunny'.

Royal Military
College Sandhurst,
in the 1890s

Polly Hackett

Winston spent the second part of his Sandhurst break, interrupted by one of his perennial bouts of flu, with a young lady he liked to describe as 'the beautiful Polly Hackett' (more often called Molly) at her aunt Lady Hindlip's home in Worcestershire, all the while scheming with his mother as to how to evade his father's express wishes and get himself posted to the cavalry.

This was a young man with astonishing global ambitions. Even at just 16 he had been recorded by Doctor Felix Salmon as announcing, 'I intend to go to Sandhurst and afterwards to join a regiment of Hussars in India. Of course it is not my intention to become a mere professional soldier. I only wish to gain some experience. Someday I shall be a statesman as my father was before me.'

Jennie was clearly complicit in Winston's ambition. She understood both her son's frailties and her husband's increasing irrationality, was herself a fine rider and, of course, was having the steamy affair with the Grand National-winning Count Kinsky. Whilst staying in London the previous November with his Aunt Leonie, Winston had met the dashing Colonel John Brabazon, the commanding officer of the 4th Hussars: 'How I wish I was going into his regiment,' he had immediately written to his mother.

Being Churchill, and one of the greatest networkers ever born, he would not leave it at that. 'I have written to Colonel Brabazon,' he now wrote to his mother from Hindlip Hall on 11 January 1894, 'and have stated my various arguments in favour of the cavalry regiment. I have asked him to say whether or not they are correct when he writes to you.' Winston then lists five reasons, such as an earlier commission, quicker promotions and better stations in India, before adding a sixth just for Jennie's eyes:

> *6 Sentimental advantages grouped under heading of Uniform*
> *Increased interest of a 'life among horse' etc.*
> *Advantages of riding over walk*
> *Advantages of joining a regiment some of whose officers you*
> *know. i.e. 4th Hussars*

At Sandhurst, Winston turned over a 'new leaf', and began to win Lord Randolph round. Churchill senior got Mr Bain, his bookseller, to send military books to the young cadet, which his son dutifully read and then commented on, in letters which also kept up a keen interest in his father's activities on the political and racing fronts. 'I am sure I shall be mentally, morally and physically better for my course here,' had been his splendidly politic declaration on the opening day of his course, signing off, 'Hoping you will write to me and send me some money for myself.'

Lord Randolph had already been mellowing, however, as is shown by the letter he'd written to his mother Frances, the Dowager Duchess, the previous autumn after taking his son down to stay with his friend and supporter Lord Nathan 'Natty' Rothschild at Tring Park, the huge house in Buckinghamshire which often hosted important guests as well as Natty's son and heir Walter Rothschild. Walter's obsession with wild animals extended to keeping a fully grown wolf that terrorised the local village, and to driving a coach pulled by four zebras up to the gates of Buckingham Palace, where Queen Alexandra risked the loss of a finger by patting one of them on the muzzle. Winston had proved a model guest, and Lord Randolph was impressed. 'He was much smartened up,' he wrote. 'The people at Tring took a great deal of notice of him, but he was very quiet and nice-mannered. Sandhurst has done wonders for him.'

Walter Rothschild and his team of zebras

It was Lord Randolph, then, the father who is always spoken of as having done little for his son, who, in an act of interested and informed parenthood, arranged for Winston to have those riding lessons in Hyde Park. Even better, he arranged for him to have them with one of the most charismatic riding masters ever to stand in the ring and shout out well-oiled lines like, 'I haven't seen anyone sit as badly as this since they tied a straw dummy on for the pantomime!' Step forward Captain Charles Henry Burt.

The uncompromising Captain would have been 42 when Winston was entrusted to his care. Born in 1852, he served almost ten years in the ranks before being promoted to Riding Master in June 1881 with an honorary title. Even now, but most especially then, riding masters offer a unique place amongst physical instructors in their ability to humiliate their pupils as they circle round them in the riding school. For it's one thing to wobble weakly on one leg in a Pilates class, or to dumbly plonk yet another easy forehand into the net; quite another to stay on board a large and unfamiliar horse as you attempt strange and apparently dangerous manoeuvres.

It is now more than 50 years ago that I spent a fortnight at the mercy of what was probably by the standards of Churchill's day a mild ex-military martinet called Fraser McMaster, at Colonel Joe Dudgeon's Burton Hall riding school outside Dublin. Brought up in Gloucestershire, with father, uncle and grandfather all proud MFH (Master of Fox Hounds), I would by then have done infinitely more hunting than Churchill, plenty of it with the Heythrop, but I remember my riding school inadequacy still. You may not be able to make the horse circle or jump as required, but the instructor knows the horse can and, which is far worse, if you fail, he can double the humiliation by putting someone else on it who will make everything look simple. With the right horse, basic riding is incredibly easy. All you have to do is sit in the saddle and let the horse carry you along. If you are reasonably fit and fearless, which the 1892 Public Schools Fencing champion certainly was when not afflicted by flu, boils, toothache or other assorted accidents, you can soon gallop around with reasonable effectiveness. But with an unwilling horse, the situation is dramatically different, for being able to make a difficult horse do difficult things requires layers of expertise, and they are best built from the bottom up.

First you have to understand the basic mechanics of the animal beneath you, and appreciate how it reacts to the shifts of your body, the pressure of the leg, the pull on the bit. That's best done initially without stirrups as, riding like that, your contact with the horse is more complete, if also less secure, not to mention comfortable. Walk across to Knightsbridge Barracks nowadays and you will still see recruits grappling with such problems. But while to outsiders today's circling manoeuvres may seem fairly hazardous, and the instructors pretty fearsome, modern standards will have softened both the methods and the language with which Captain Burt would have used to set his pupil up for Sandhurst.

Behind Lord Randolph's generosity was a more simple fact. For all the reports of his changed appearance and increasing frailty – a year earlier he had returned from a gold-prospecting trip to South Africa with a long, straggly prophet's beard to leave many already expecting the worst – he still loved to get in the saddle himself. In January 1894 he had just 12 months to live, yet here he was writing to 'Dearest Jennie' from Ireland about a wonderful day with the Meath Hunt in the countryside north of Dublin. 'I was very lucky yesterday,' he wrote,

> *as Mr Neil gave me his best horse and a better one I never rode. In the little sport we had I took him over some enormous jumps. He was beautifully bred, beautiful manners and a beautiful*

galloper and jumper. Paddy and Mr Neil were surprised and delighted with the way I showed him off. I felt in very good nerve and in great confidence with the horse. I very nearly tumbled off at a very nasty place but recovered myself.

Not surprisingly, Randolph went on to say that he was quite stiff, as he hadn't hunted for a while.

February 1894 saw the start of Winston's second term at Sandhurst, and the first in which riding was on the official curriculum. Although cadets at the Royal Military Academy were ultimately destined for a particular regiment, which might be the cavalry, the infantry or the engineers, all of them received the same wide-ranging military education, and with riding as central to society as it still was in the late nineteenth century, riding was central to the curriculum. As we have seen, Winston had ridden a fair bit, but he was anything but an expert. He may have galloped across Newmarket Heath, but he had never been hunting until he went to the Boxing Day meet of the Heythrop when staying with Sunny that Christmas. Official riding schools like the one at Sandhurst can be demanding even for those who are quite advanced, so the 12 lessons he had just received from Captain Burt could not have been more priceless.

That February 1894 Winston followed an eight-page letter for Lord Randolph's 45th birthday with another one from Sandhurst. 'The riding here is most interesting,' he wrote, 'and I got great "kudos" from the instructors and have been put at the head of the ride. It was quite worthwhile getting up early and taking those lessons.' This prompted a 'Dear Winny', reply from his father, complete with two sovereigns for Captain Burt, and one each for the groom and 'the man who got your breakfast'.

WSC plays the clown

It's important to remember that for all his cockiness (after getting 'six of the best' from the head boy at Harrow he had said 'I will be a greater man than you' – and promptly got two more), Winston was at this stage still something of a physical weed. He may have entranced Molly Hackett as he and she 'strolled Bond Street way' the day before his Knightsbridge lesson, but he was far from an imposing physical specimen: when he got to Sandhurst he measured just five foot six and three-quarter inches, with a puny 31-inch chest. 'I am cursed with so feeble a body that I can hardly support the fatigues of the day,' he had written to his mother within a fortnight of enrolment, 'but I suppose I shall get stronger during my stay here.' A month later there was an even more miserable note:

I had to run three-quarters of a mile with rifles and accoutrements the other day, and I had to be helped off parade by a couple of sergeants at the end of it and have been bad ever since. Just the same as when I took the Turkish Bath. I have been to see the doctor and he says there is nothing wrong except that my heart does not seem to be very strong.

To become the man who had the courage and toughness to save the world, Churchill had to conquer that feebleness. Not only was he going to make himself into a good rider, but four days after that first Boxing Day meet he was also out hunting and jumping a second time. He was going to use all his emerging powers of energy and persuasion to get himself into the cavalry so that he could seek youthful glory on horseback.

A month later the devoted but scheming son was at it again, with a gem of a letter to his father which included thanks for a book he had been sent, praise for his father's politics ('I read your speech carefully and thought it excellent'), and reports of continued equestrian achievement: 'the riding is going very well and they have taken to making me ride the difficult horses as soon as their other riders come off. So far all has been very successful and Major Hodgkins, the Riding Master, is very civil and takes great pains with me.' Considering the Major's methods included the cracking of whips and the firing of pistols close to the horses, Churchill's civility was a tribute to the young cadet, as it also must have been to Captain Burt's earlier grounding.

Lord Randolph's responses were not always too generous – one letter after Winston damaged a gold watch he had been given is preserved at Blenheim as a public exhibit of how fraught the relationship could be. Yet the compliments and the racing and riding news continued, and mixed amongst them were subtle straws to see if the wind could be changing on the infantry/cavalry issue. Winston would feed in news of how impressed he had been by the 4th Hussars when he'd visited Colonel Brabazon at Aldershot, how smart the Colonel had looked when he came to Sandhurst, and how the Hussars had been the most gleamingly efficient of all the troops on parade at the Grand Review.

Winston's agonising over his thwarted ambitions comes through in a much more open letter he wrote to his mother about Colonel Brabazon and the Aldershot Review: 'How I wish I were going into the 4th rather than those old Rifles,' he wrote.

> It would not cost a penny more [as we have seen, Churchill was wrong there] and the regiment goes to India in three years which is just right for me. I hate the Infantry – in which physical weaknesses will render me useless on service and the only thing I am showing an aptitude for athletically – riding – will be no good to me.

> Furthermore of all the regiments in the army the Rifles is slowest for promotion. However it is not much good writing down all these cogent arguments – but if I pass high at the end of the term I will tackle Papa on the subject.

But though Lord Randolph was still going to Epsom to watch his host Lord Rosebery's Ladas win the Derby, the former Chancellor was already very publicly losing the plot. 'There was no retirement,' Lord Rosebery himself was to write of his friend, 'no concealment, he died by inches in public.' As early as March 1894, Lord Randolph's delivery as he spoke in the House of Commons was so bad that Arthur Balfour sat head bowed. Three weeks before the Derby, the writer, poet and Arab horse enthusiast Wilfrid Scawen Blunt met Randolph after a long absence and reported, 'he is terribly altered poor fellow, having some disease, paralysis I suppose, which affects his speech so that it is painful to listen to him. He makes prodigious efforts to express himself but these are only too visible.'

Jennie, as we have seen, was sympathetic to her son's ambition to the point of collusion, but she had problems enough on her plate. Her husband was obviously dying, and her immediate plans were to take Randolph on a make or break tour to America, Canada and the Far East. Moreover, Count Kinsky had said he would wait for her, but his family wanted him to marry a wealthy young Austrian to ensure a successor. Winston would just have to buckle down in the saddle and hope for the best – or in this case the very unhappy worst – to happen in time.

Rotten Row, Hyde Park at the end of the 19th century

To his eternal credit that is what he did. He did go to the Derby, Ascot and the Eclipse Stakes at Sandown, but he also became increasingly paternal to the now 14-year-old Jack. He took his brother on a Brussels-to-Zermatt-to-Milan-to-Vienna tour in August, and all the time continued a touchingly intimate correspondence with Mrs 'Woomanly' Everest whose cause he had championed when his grandmother had 'economised' and dismissed her from 50 Grosvenor Square. The 'feeble frame', meanwhile, had become tough enough to ride the 14 miles from Windsor to Sandhurst after dining with the racing figure Lord Wolverton following Royal Ascot. When he wrote to his mother at the end of July he reported he was riding in Rotten Row every day – as well as boasting that he and Molly Hackett had been, 'all alone', to visit Harrow.

That letter also revealed that he had tried again with his father on the question of the cavalry. Lord Randolph may have arranged for his son to have extra riding lessons, but on this he was immovable, and in an otherwise very civil reply datelined 'Hotel Del Monte, California', Lord Randolph turned the prospect down flat: 'I could never sanction such a change.' But Winston Churchill was not one for giving up easily, and he had not been back at Sandhurst a week when he clearly signalled his intentions.

'The riding has begun also,' he wrote to his mother, now en route to Yokohama in Japan,

> and I am working hard at it. I should like nothing better than to win the Riding Prize. My only chance of persuading Papa to let me go into the cavalry is to do something of that sort. If I take 'Honours' very high on the list in passing out or win the Riding Prize I shall broach the subject again, but till then the future is very gloomy. At Sandown this year [Eclipse Stakes] the Duke of Cambridge spoke to me. He said, 'You're at Sandhurst aren't you? Do you like it?' I said yes and Col. Brab [Colonel Brabazon] who was there said, 'Going into my regiment, eh.' The Duke said, 'Oh I am very glad.' So really he had forgotten all about the 60th.

Churchill may not have done that much riding before he got to Sandhurst, but now, to impress his father sufficiently to finally change his mind, he had decided to aim for nothing less than the highest accolade awarded for it there.

'I went out with our paper chase yesterday and had a couple of falls,' he wrote to his mother proudly.

> In the first my horse pecked on landing and fell and in the second I turned a corner at much too rapid a pace and so came to grief. I am not at all hurt – which I consider most wonderful as I was galloped over both times. I do love this kind of riding.

*You know how little I have hunted. I don't think anything would
stop me if I had a good horse.*

*As it is these hirelings are very uncertain and fall down as often
as not – when jumping. I am pinching and scraping to hire a
better animal for a month and any contribution you might be
inclined to send would be thankfully received.*

*I do not think there is anything I would rather do than hunt –
I mean as far as pleasure is concerned. We were about 17 last
Wednesday and as we are all very keen – we go pretty hard.
Nearly everyone had a fall of some sort.*

This was the moment in his career that later spawned a most
splendid riff in *My Early Life*, with which I used to bombard my
parents to get their wonderful if sometimes rather nerve-shredded
support for my own steeplechasing ambitions.

'Horses were the greatest of my pleasures at Sandhurst,' it begins.

*I and the group in which I moved spent all our money on
hiring horses from the very excellent local livery stables.
We ran up bills on the strength of future commissions. We
organised point-to-points and even a steeplechase in the park
of a friendly grandee, and bucketed gaily about the countryside.
And here I say to parents, 'Don't give your son money. As
far as you can afford it, give him horses.' No one ever came
to grief – except honourable grief – through riding horses.
No hour of life is lost that is spent in the saddle. Young men
have often been ruined through owning horses, or through
backing horses, but never through riding them; unless of course
they break their necks, which, taken at the gallop, is a very
good death to die.*

Churchill was 55 when he wrote that, and you can detect the
warming of the hands at the memories of the boldness of youth. But
it's not too fanciful to also discern the clenched jaw of a politician
then out of office but ready, when the day came ten years later, to gallop at the highest fences in our history. For let's not pretend this was
some one-track horsey youth. The 'paper chase' letter to his mother
quoted previously may have included the programme for an Eton v
Harrow Pony Race Meeting in which Winston was a steward and rode
in the second race, but it did not start with saddle talk: it began with
acute observations about the Sino-Japanese war over Korea, in which
the Japanese had forced the surrender of the large Chinese garrison
at Pyongyang. 'I take the greatest interest in the operations of both
the fleets and the armies,' he wrote. 'Anything so brilliant as the night
attack on Ping Yang is hard to find in modern war.'

A lot of ambitions were racing around the young cadet's gingery head, and in November 1894 Churchill led an energetic protest against the – ultimately successful – efforts of the so called 'Purity Campaign' to close the bars at the Empire Theatre, Leicester Square. Dubbing the campaigners 'Prudes on the Prowl', he not only wrote a letter to the *Westminster Gazette*, but it was on this issue that Winston made his very first public speech, standing on the debris of the canvas partitions shutting off the bars.

The news from the Far East, however, where Jennie had taken Randolph, was getting worse, and after Dr Roose had told him the full gravity of his father's illness, a warm arm was put around his younger brother:

> *November 29th*
> *My Darling Jack,*
>
> *Papa and Mamma are coming home and will be at Monte Carlo by the end of December, so we shall be able to go out and see them. The doctors think that if he keeps perfectly quiet he may yet get well – though he will never be able to go into Politics again. Keep your spirits up and write to –*
>
> *Your loving brother*
> *WINSTON*

Sandhurst, another view

10879   ROYAL MILITARY COLLEGE.

The Military Academy's final exams were coming, and doing well in them was very much part of the plan, as well as a vain hope to revive Lord Randolph. 'Winston is I think working very hard at Sandhurst,' Jack wrote to his father, with details that would later have great significance,

and thinks he might pass out high. He says the riding has come much ruffer [sic], such as mounting and dismounting at the gallop. He says he found it very difficult at first as it was a new thing and no one had practised it before. He found he was quite as good as anyone else.

Just six years later the ability to mount at the gallop would save Winston's life in South Africa.

By now Lord Randolph had less than six weeks to live, and Winston must have known that communication was futile, so you have to admire the desperation in the revealing detail he includes in his report on the riding exam. It is worth quoting the first part in full:

My Dearest Father,

You cannot think how delighted we all are to hear of your return for Christmas in Europe. It is splendid to be able to write to you and feel that this letter will reach you in only a few short days – instead of months.

The Riding Examinations took place on Friday. First of all – all the cadets were examined who pass out this term – 127 in all. Then 15 were picked to compete together for the prize. I was one of those and in the afternoon we all rode – the General, Col. Gough of the Greys and Capt Byng, 10th Hussars, Judges – with dozens of officers and many more cadets as spectators. This RIDING FOR THE PRIZE is considered a great honour and the cadets take a great interest in it.

Well we rode – jumped with & without stirrups & without reins – hands behind the back and other tricks. Then five were weeded out leaving only ten of us. Then we went into the field & rode over the numerous fences several times. Six more were weeded out leaving only four in. I was wild with excitement and rode I think better than I have ever done before, but failed to win the prize by one mark, being 2nd with 199 out of 200 marks.

I am awfully pleased with the result, which in a place where everyone rides means a great deal, as I shall have to ride before the Duke and also it makes it easy to pick regts when the Colonels know you can ride. I hope you will be pleased.

Out of his whole year of 127 cadets at the Royal Military Academy, Winston had come second in nothing other than riding, and had dropped just a single mark out of a possible maximum. It was the greatest achievement of his life so far. He may have won a declamation prize and a fencing championship; he may have made a public speech in Leicester Square. Having only ranked 95th overall when arriving at Sandhurst he may have risen to 20th on leaving, but nothing compared to this. Surely his father, in hiring Captain Burt to give his son those priceless lessons in Hyde Park, had played his part. Winston had wanted to show enough courage and physicality and judgement to guarantee his future in the cavalry. Nothing could stop him now.

The forlorn, shaking figure of his father returned to 50 Grosvenor Square on Christmas Eve, and died on a snowy London night exactly a month later on 24 January 1895. His had been a brilliant, if flawed, career; he had been a demanding, dismissive but probably well-intentioned parent. His decline had been swift and dreadful. 'Health and balance', concluded his nephew and godson Shane Leslie, 'were denied to a brain still winged with genius and weighted with ambitions. The collapse of an aeroplane in mid-air is always more terrible than the overturning of a hackney cab in the street. Randolph fell from meteoric heights, and men wondered as much as they pitied.'

Amidst all their grief, Winston and Jennie went to work. As early as 6 February 1895 a letter arrived from the Duke of Cambridge, authorising Winston's change from the 60th Rifles to the 4th Hussars. The proud subaltern was on his way to the command of Colonel Brabazon.

'When I passed out of Sandhurst into the world,' Churchill wrote, 'it opened like Aladdin's cave.' And, since he was going into a cavalry regiment, many of those wonders would be coming at the gallop.

HOUSE WHERE LORD RANDOLPH CHURCHILL DIED, 50, GROSVENOR SQUARE.

05

THE BOLD HUSSAR, 1895

"I rode on Thursday in my first steeplechase – at the Aldershot races," Winston had written to Jack in words that hardly smack of those of a co-conspirator. "One of our fellows had two horses running in the Subalterns' Cup and could get no one to ride the second. So I said I would and did. It was very exciting and there is no doubt about it being pretty dangerous. I had never jumped a regulation fence before and they are pretty big things as you know."

Previous page: WSC commissioned in the 4th Hussars

The last time I rode at Tweseldown was my final race before turning professional. I thought I was the bee's knees, and pulled my dark goggles down whilst walking round the paddock. The once classy but now cunning old horse called Plummer's Plain got the picture and dumped me in the first open ditch. On 20 March 1895, at what was then termed Aldershot Races, the 20-year-old Winston Churchill did rather better by finishing third amidst four fellow officers in the 18-fence, two-mile-five-furlong 4th Hussars Subalterns' Cup. It was the first and last time he rode in a steeplechase. But it could have finished him.

Not physically. For, despite his family's fearfulness and his own protestations of danger, to sit on an experienced jumper over the steeplechase course in such a small field should have been well within the compass of a fit little subaltern who had spent the last year energetically practising all forms of equitation. No, the danger, for someone already nursing lofty dreams of public office, was much graver than that. The race was a 'fix' and if exposed, could have drummed him out of polite society.

As it was, the race triggered a press vendetta, and even questions in Parliament, when the scandal erupted fully eleven months after the event, with the publication of a single, staid, 60-word paragraph in the utterly formal pages of the *Racing Calendar*. On the surface the announcement may have seemed a dull read, but in racing terms it was dynamite. Since no further official information has ever surfaced, I commend you, as the lawyers say, to the phrase 'certain irregularities' in the first sentence.

RACING CALENDAR
20 February 1896
[Exactly 11 months after the race in question]

The attention of the Stewards of the National Hunt Committee having been called to certain irregularities in respect of the 4th Hussars Subalterns' Cup, run at the Cavalry Brigade Meeting at Aldershot, 1895 [see Steeple Chases Past, 1895 p. 78], the race has been declared null and void and all the horses who took part in the same are perpetually disqualified for all races under National Hunt Rules.

What 'irregularities'? And why had all the horses been 'warned off' for life, but no action taken against the five dashing subalterns who rode them? Answers, down the years, have come there none, and so I have to take you through the facts as presented. At first sight they do not make pretty reading.

The 4th Hussars Subalterns' Cup was run on the Wednesday, the second day of the two-day Cavalry Brigade Meeting which, as the name suggests, and as still now happens with the Grand Military and Royal Artillery Meetings at Sandown, was predominantly for military personnel, but also open to professional riders, and run under official National Hunt rules. This is crucial, because it meant that Churchill's race was open to public betting. So while the Subalterns' Cup ranked fairly low amongst steeplechasing fare – little more, in status, and certainly less, in competitiveness, than many a point-to-point – it was an event on which plenty of money could be won or lost. Particularly if you knew that a horse called Surefoot was not what it was supposed to be, but something rather better.

Surefoot, or what was supposed to be Surefoot, duly ran home a six length winner at 6-1, much to the pleasure of those who had backed him, and to the dismay of those who had bet Lady Margaret down to 5-4 favourite following her impressive victory the previous day. The 2-1 second favourite Dolly Do Little was a faller under Henry Walker, Tartina and rider Reggie Barnes were last, and Winston's mount Traveller a distant third to Lady Margaret, ridden by Albert Savory, who owned both her and Traveller.

Horses are not machines: such unexpected results happen all the time and, to one rider at least, this was a red-letter day. 'Everybody in the regiment is pretty pleased at my riding,' Winston wrote proudly to his brother, 'more especially as I came third. They thought it very sporting. I thought so too. It has done me a lot of good here, and I think I may say I am popular with everybody.'

A year later the suggestions were of a very different nature. 'The circumstances of this race were of a most extraordinary character,' wrote the MP Henry Labouchere in his feared and often scurrilous weekly *Truth*, after the official statement voiding the event and banning all five runners had been published. 'The perpetual disqualification of the horses of all these officers points to some irregularity of a serious description, and if I am correctly informed as to the nature of the irregularity, no censure could be too strong for the conduct of those directly implicated.'

Labouchere was an odd sort of dog, but a dangerous opponent. At Cambridge he lost a fortune betting at Newmarket, and was denied his degree for cheating in exams. In the Diplomatic Service he was sacked for responding to a new posting in Buenos Aires by writing, 'I beg to state that, if residing in Baden Baden, I can fulfil those duties, I shall be pleased to accept the appointment.' In Parliament for 30 years, he was on the radical side of the Liberal Party, yet was virulently anti-Semitic, anti-feminist, and so homophobic that it was his 1885 'Labouchere Amendment' that led to the imprisonment of Oscar Wilde ten years later.

Labouchere was not one to leave a bone if he thought there was more meat on it, and this one had enough to take other allegations about the subalterns involved in the Aldershot affair all the way to questions in Parliament in the June of 1896. At the core would be accusations that in two cases, one before Churchill's arrival, the subalterns had bullied a fellow officer out of the regiment. In the first, Albert Savory and Reggie Barnes had horse-troughed a luckless aspirant called George Hodge, and in the second, all five riders in the Subalterns' Cup had organised a dinner in London at which Churchill had made a condemnatory speech where one Allan Bruce was told he was not wanted. Parliament would not condemn, but Labouchere kept up his attacks into the autumn. 'At the very time,' he wrote in *Truth* on 22 October, 'that this precious gang met to inform Mr Bruce the 4th Hussars really could not have him, five of them (including the ring-leader) were fresh from the coup which resulted in the defeat of a hot favourite in the betting.'

By October 1896 Churchill was majoring in polo at his barracks in Bangalore, but quite how deep these allegations bit is best seen from a vital letter to his mother on 12 November.

> *Mr Labouchere's last article in* Truth *is really too hot for words. I fail to see any other course than a legal action. He distinctly says that five of us – mentioning my name – were implicated in a 'coup' to obtain money by malpractice on the Turf. You must not allow this to go unchallenged, as it would be fatal to any future in public life for me. Indeed, I dare say I should be exposed to attacks even on the grounds of having helped turn out Bruce. This racing matter is much more serious. You know the facts – so does Colonel Brabazon. The NH* [National Hunt] *Committee furnished the WO* [War Office] *with a letter vindicating us from any charge of dishonesty or dishonourable behaviour. A copy of this can be seen at Messrs Weatherbys* [the official secretariat of the ruling Jockey Club]. *Consult a good lawyer – not Lewis – he is Labby's lawyer. Let him see the articles in* Truth: *furnish him with the actual facts and follow his advice.*

Sadly, no record of the claimed letter of vindication has been found, and while the Army ended the case without censure, and Labouchere's campaign finally closed down, none of the suggested legal action was taken. Of course, all this was to be raised, and finally dissolved, many months after Churchill's ride at Aldershot, but his conduct in both the Bruce and the racing episodes, extremely unbecoming though it was in the first, most of all reflects an insecure eagerness to win the approval of his fellow cavalrymen.

When our own son went into his regiment from Sandhurst, he had already been an academic and sporting success right through his schooldays, and still had two devoted if slightly nervous parents. For Winston, with his father now a mythical hero with political wrongs to be righted, and a mother who was much more ally than nanny, this was the time to prove himself a man. As we have seen from his excited letter to Jack, he saw being brave on horseback as a central part of the process. Indeed, whatever one's views on the Bruce case, the best defence against Winston's collusion in the 'Surefoot scandal' is the sheer naivety of his reactions at the time.

'I rode on Thursday in my first steeplechase – at the Aldershot races,' Winston had written to Jack in words that hardly smack of those of a co-conspirator.

> *One of our fellows had two horses running in the Subalterns'*
> *Cup and could get no one to ride the second. So I said I would*
> *and did. It was very exciting and there is no doubt about it*
> *being pretty dangerous. I had never jumped a regulation fence*
> *before and they are pretty big things as you know. I rode under*
> *the name of Spencer as of course it was all put in the papers.*
> *No one will know however as I adopted a 'nom de guerre'.*

There is a delightful verve in the innocence of it all. For the first time you ride in a steeplechase is truly a leap into a different world. As the starter drops his flag the walking horse becomes a galloping rocket with you above it. The fences sweep towards you and it soars you over. It's the most athletic thing you have ever done: half a ton of horse jumping five foot high and 30 foot long and landing spring-heeled ready for the next obstacle up ahead.

Tweseldown was closed even as a point-to-point course in 2013, but the outline of the track remains, and walking it again I remembered the sweep down away from the cars (carriages in Churchill's day) at the top of the hill, and the long run beside the woodland with the big ditch at the bottom. Then the final swing back to the finish with the people shouting. It's heady stuff for any beginner, and even if you were only plodding on to be a distant third, the fulfilment for 'Mr Spencer' would be manhood-plus.

A hundred and twenty years is a long distance from which to cast judgement on what happened in that 'voided' Subalterns' Cup. But if anyone is to be put into the frame for what happened at Aldershot it would probably be Albert Savory, the rider of the beaten favourite, and as he got killed, as yet unmarried, five years later in the Boer War, there are no descendants to defend him. Tempting as it is to try and spawn a CHURCHILL IN FIXED RACE headline, Winston does not look much of a suspect to me, and I speak with some experience. For back at Chepstow in 1963, my own self-congratulatory delight at winning a first race over hurdles in what I thought was a power-packed finish was somewhat tempered by the later news that the rider of the second had been had up for not trying.

Churchill may have been second in the Sandhurst riding class, but he was a greenhorn compared to the likes of Albert Savory and Reggie Barnes. He had hardly been with them a month, and the others were not just senior to him in years, they were infinitely tougher physically and more seasoned in the saddle. They were already accomplished steeplechase riders and polo players, and Reggie Barnes had even hunted a pack of hounds when stationed in County Cork. When Churchill joined the 4th Hussars he would need to take his physicality and riding to a whole new dimension.

Looking back 30 years, he wrote that his early days in the Aldershot riding school under a new tyrant called 'Jocko' 'exceeded in severity anything I had previously experienced in military equitation'. The pages of *My Early Life* grant a wry indulgence at his young self, as he lists the challenges and humiliations awaiting the young officer going through the mincer alongside the lower rank recruits:

> *Mounting and dismounting from a bare-backed horse at the trot or canter; jumping a high bar without stirrups or even a saddle, sometimes with hands clasped behind one's back; jogging at a fast trot with nothing but the horse's hide between your knees brought their inevitable share of mishaps. Many a time did I pick myself up shaken and sore from the riding-school tan and don again my little gold-braided pork pie cap, fastened on the chin by a bootlace strap, with what dignity I could command, while twenty recruits grinned furtively but delightedly to see their Officer suffering the same misfortunes which it was their lot so frequently to undergo.*

Writing at the time, he acknowledged a greater frailty. 'The riding school is frightfully severe and I suffer terribly from stiffness,' he wrote to his mother after a couple of days.

> *But with hot baths and massage, I hope soon to be better. At present I can hardly walk. I have however been moved up into the 2nd Class recruits which is extremely good. These horses are very different from the Sandhurst screws. Rather too broad I think for me – and I am rather worried about my old strain: Sundry queer pains have manifested themselves, which may or may not be the outcome of the rest of the stiffness.*

A couple of days later he is still struggling when he writes,

> *The riding school here is a terribly severe business. Two hours – trotting out on a fiery steed much too wide for me & a slippery saddle with no stirrups. The result is I am so fearfully stiff I cannot walk and am much swollen. However there is nothing to it but to go on and work it off, a very painful process.*

The young man who wants to be a proper cavalryman protests too much. For even though I can feel my thigh muscles wincing at the thought of two hours without stirrups on an unfamiliar horse and an uncomfortable saddle, there is still a fair degree of the young aristocrat 'wuss' about this as Winston lists his daily schedule:

THE RIDING SCHOOL, *(continued)*

15

" Swords "

Awkward if one loses one's stirrup jumping.

Don't stick your toes out like a Hinfantry Hadjutant, Sir! "

Sergeant Chamberlain

Major Higgins   *" Eyes   right —   Salute ! "*

By your front —Draw Swords !   *Buckling on the sabre*

By your centre —Return Swords !

7.30	*Called*
7.45	*Breakfast in bed, papers letters etc .*
8.45	*Riding School two hours,*
10.45	*Hot baths and massage.*

Tell that to anyone getting up in the dark, mucking out and then riding two lots before breakfast, and they will laugh out loud – and that's before we get to the bit where he says, 'I have a servant, willing, hard-working but quite untrained.' You could take the boy out of the palace, but could you take the palace out of the boy? The story of this 21st and crucial year of Churchill's life is how the 'feeble-framed' boy grew into the jutting-jawed, if still baby-faced, little man, whilst only increasing his access to palace-style connections.

To be fair, it is not easy to mix the two. I remember what it was like moving from the privileges of public school and an Oxford education into the harsher college of the jockeys' changing room, where others had mindsets and muscles so obviously harder than one's own. You might be no match for them, but at least you were sharing their dangers, and there was even an 'initiation-rite' pride in the disasters that lurk for everyone – like a horse going out through the wing. 'I have had the misfortune to smash myself up while trying a horse on the steeplechase course,' wrote Churchill to his mother in Paris on 12 March, where she was now comfortably installed in the Avenue Kleber.

The animal refused and swerved – I tried to cram him in – and
he took the wings. Very nearly did I break my leg – but as it is
I am only bruised and very stiff. I shall be out again in two or
three days. In the meantime everybody is very kind – so kind
indeed that I am sure I have made a very good impression –
(why should I not?).

Such statements can unnerve un-versed parents, even some as
resilient and as hunting bold as Jennie Churchill. Within the week the
son was back trying to play down the extent of his no doubt previously
played-up injury and, on the assumption she would not be back from
Paris too soon, shamelessly deceiving his mother about his imminent
debut onto the steeplechasing scene.

I think if you will let me say – that you take rather an extreme
view of steeplechasing – when you call it at once 'idiotic' and
'fatal'. Everybody here rides one or other of their chargers in the
different military races which are constantly held. Of course
this year I cannot ride, but I hope to do so next year.

In fact I rather think you are expected to do something that way
– ride in the Regimental races at least. However I shall see you
long before I can ride and you can discuss it with me.

There does not seem to be an exact record of Jennie Churchill's
reaction to the news of 'Mr Spencer''s ride in the Subalterns' Cup,
but her own mother's death on 2 April is likely to have assumed more
importance anyway. What's more, after the traumas of Randolph's
final descent had been compounded by Count Kinsky conceding to
family pressure and marrying an Austrian heiress, Jennie was treating
herself to some 'Merry Widow' time in Paris. There she formed a relationship with the great Irish-American orator Bourke Cockran, who
within a few months was to become a crucial influence on one of the
greatest ever speakers in the English tongue. Whatever her reaction
to Winston's racing news in March, she can only have been pleased
with the growing confidence her son was showing after recovering
from another accident a month later.
    'I am very fit and my leg is healing slowly – and is nearly well,'
he wrote.

I rode in that point-to-point after all on Tuesday with a big
bandage on. It was nothing like a steeplechase – being only
a hunting run – and not a fast one – but it was a ripping line –
49 fences. Out of 13 started only five got round – I was fourth
being beautifully mounted. No one was hurt in the least – though
more than half took tosses. It was not the least dangerous and
did me a lot of good in the regiment. All the subalterns rode.

There was a crucial phrase at the end of that letter: 'I am having a really good time and enjoying life immensely.' Barely two months into his life as an Hussar he had begun to crack it but, as ever with him, that produced more activity, not less. And that, as it involved horses and someone as congenitally spendthrift as Winston Churchill, required money. His cavalry officer's pay was £120 a year. In that same 'point-to-point' letter he had sent a detailed costing of his initial outlay for uniform, saddlery, boots, horses and subscriptions. It had come to £653.11.0 – more than four years' pay. Sounds like a case for the Distressed Gentlefolks Association – but that wasn't formed until 1897.

Of course, Jennie and Winston were as bad as each other. A few years later he was to write to her: 'Speaking quite frankly on the subject, there is no doubt that we are both – you & I – equally thoughtless – spendthrift and extravagant. We both know what is good and we both like to have it.' And whilst phrases like 'desperately hard-up' are frequently used, so are ones like 'and then as regards the polo ponies...' Churchill may have famously said, 'We are damned poor,' but an annual allowance of £500 from his father's will was no more penury than his mother's £5,000. Both of them shamelessly ducked and dived with creditors and relations, whilst gaily proceeding with the lifestyle to which they liked to be accustomed.

And what style it was. Churchill's new mentor was his commanding officer Colonel John 'Bwab' Brabazon, so nicknamed for his inability to pronounce his Rs and the oft-told story of his altercation with the station master at Aldershot.

'Where's my twain?'

'Gone, Colonel.'

'Gone? Then bwing another.'

Thirty-five years later his figure still glowed in the then young subaltern's memory. 'He was one of the brightest military stars in London society,' Churchill wrote in *My Early Life*.

> *A close, lifelong friendship between him and the Prince of Wales at Court, in the Clubs, on the racecourse, in the hunting field, he was accepted as a most distinguished figure. Now in his prime his appearance was magnificent. His clean-cut, symmetrical features, his bright grey eyes and strong jaw, were shown to the best advantage by a moustache which the Kaiser might well have taken as his unattainable ordeal. To all this he added the airs and manner of the dandies of the generation before his own, and an inability real or affected to pronounce the letter 'R'. Apt and experienced in conversation, his remarkable personality was never at a loss in any company, polite or otherwise.*

With this star in his firmament, Lieutenant Churchill was hardly likely to start buying clothes in a charity shop, and certainly not to cut down on the horses – and he didn't. Quite apart from all his astonishing, already harboured 'man of destiny' ambitions, he intended to cut his own path in society, on horseback and on the turf and to leave no connection, family or otherwise, untouched in the pursuit of it. To this end nothing could be better than the wedding, on 30 April 1895, of the wealthy American 'Duchess Lily', the widowed second wife of his Uncle Blandford, the 8th Duke of Marlborough, to that ultimate Victorian hero Lord William Beresford, horseman, race rider, pig sticker, and winner of the VC in the Zulu Wars at Ulundi.

Colonel Brabazon, WSC's charismatic commanding officer

Ever since Winston got into Sandhurst, Duchess Lily had been promising him a good horse, and in recent months had even talked to Colonel Brabazon about getting it with a generous budget of £200. But, despite all her nephew's promptings, no actual purchase had yet been made, and 'Duchess Lily' and 'Lord Bill''s wedding reception was clearly the place to strike. Winston's letter to his mother is as brilliant an example of his then wants as you could wish to see. It also demonstrates that he was not exactly moving in impoverished circles, nor planned, despite claiming to be 'absolutely at the end of my funds', to cut down any time soon.

> I went to the Duchess Lily's wedding, everyone was there. A most excellent breakfast which must have cost a great deal – and crowds to eat it – were the chief feature. 'Lord Bill' at once broached the topic of the charger & said I was to get a real good one – the best that could be got. That is however in Brab's hands and I can't hustle HIM.

> After the wedding I went down to Newmarket to see the Two Thousand [Guineas]. My Captain – a charming man – who has a good many horses in training there – gave me dinner – and I breakfasted with young Sherwood. I saw the whole world in the stand. The Prince asked after you as did many others. Lady Norris – Lady Hindlip – the Wolvertons – all the Rothschilds – Sir John Delacour – Freddy Johnstone – The Old Duke, the Burtons – everyone in fact & all most civil and agreeable. I enjoyed myself very much.

Lieutenant Churchill may have been only 20, and looked barely 16, but he knew how to network, and his involvement in racing was not as an outsider. For 'young Sherwood' was Bob Sherwood, who had taken over St Gatien Stables the previous year after the unfortunate demise from apoplexy of his father, the trainer of L'Abbesse De Jouarre and others for Lord Randolph. Either on their own account, or through Lord Randolph's will, Winston and Jennie had ownership of a two-year-old in training at St Gatien. Winston had already registered racing colours similar to his father's pink and chocolate silks, and his and Jennie's 1895 correspondence has many references to the colt by Allotment out of Gervas, who was later named Gold Key.

Winston's report of his trip to see their horse on Guineas morning will ring true to owners down the ages. It is May, the season of hopefulness. The two-year-old is brought out. His coat gleams, his hooves shine, as he stands perfect outside his box. The trainer explains that he is very pleased with him, but he will take a little time to find his full potential. He will try not to give you too many words, as hostages to fortune, but he will give the firm impression that your money has been well spent (by him, remember) and will above all leave hanging in the air that most narcotic of racing thoughts – 'This could be anything...'

On 1 May 1895, it was Winston Churchill who was living the dream. 'In the morning I saw the Allotment colt,' he writes to his mother.

> *You must name him. He was very well though backward coming into training. Such a good looking animal with such promise. In a month he will be fit & if agreeable to you can be tried with some of Sherwood's horses whose form is known. Then you will know what his worth is – and what class animal he is.*

Maybe the future Gold Key would be the answer to all their financial difficulties, but from the son's closing lines one would not bank on it. 'Well, goodbye, my darling Mama – let me beg you to try and send me some little money, as it is not a case of current expenses but paying deliberately incurred liabilities.'

The hunting and steeplechasing seasons might be over, but the time for polo and for continued general riding only grew. Winston managed to get the bank to lend him £100 to buy three ponies, and within a week was writing, 'Polo progresses steadily and I am, I think, improving fast. It is the finest game in the world and I should almost be content to give up any ambition to play it well and often.'

When the Duke of Cambridge arrived at Aldershot with Prince Nasrullah Khan of Afghanistan, as part of an official visit for Britain to impress his father, the Amir Abdur Rahman (despite the latter's habit of hanging robbers up in cages and leaving them to rot), it was Lt Churchill who rode escort. For reasons of bladder control and bottom soreness it was surely an exaggeration when he wrote of 'seven hours in the saddle without dismounting or removing my busby and two more after lunch,' but it was clearly an honour to be selected.

All that was done before the much welcomed arrival of Duchess Lily's long-promised £200 quadruped, 'a magnificent animal which is said to be the finest charger in the army', and which was no doubt used for his daily rides in Windsor Park after the racing at Royal Ascot.

Churchill's search for ladies, meanwhile, was not going that well, and family life was suddenly full of sadness. His Windsor Park riding companion Lady Angela St Clair-Erskine had her cap set at Sunny Marlborough. The 'lovely Molly Hackett' had got engaged to an Edward Wilson, whose sister Muriel was invited down with the affianced pair to Aldershot, and no more seems to have been heard of the Lyric Theatre and the actress Mabel Love, with whom he had swapped photos a year back. But all that was fluff compared to the bombshell that arrived by telegram on Monday evening. Mrs Everest was dying.

The last letter from her had come two months earlier after the Subalterns' Cup excitements. 'I hope you will take care of yourself, my darling,' his adored nurse and confidante had written.

*I hear of your exploits at steeplechasing. I do so dread to hear
of it. Remember Count Kinsky broke his nose at that. It is
a dangerous pastime but I suppose you are expected to do it.
Only don't be too venturesome. Goodbye darling with much
love to you.*

I remain ever your loving old
WOOM

Winston was heartbroken. He got up to Crouch End in time to
be with her at the close. Jack got out of Harrow to attend the funeral,
and the two of them organised and inscribed a tombstone on her
grave in the City of London Cemetery in Manor Park.

In the last year, he had lost his father, his maternal grandmother
and now the lynchpin of his youth and childhood. 'I feel very despond-
ent and sad,' he wrote to his mother.

WSC, a proud subaltern

It's the third funeral I have been to within five months. I am longing for the day when you will be able to have a little house of your own and when I can really feel there is such a place as home. At present I regard the regiment entirely as my headquarters and if I go up to London for a couple of days – I always look forward to coming back to my friends and ponies here.

There was clearly a lot going on inside his head, and he needed both work and play to staunch its bubbling energy. 'I thought how odd he looked, his hair and gold lace forage cap the same colour,' said Lance Corporal Hallaway on first meeting the young lieutenant. 'I had to tell him all I knew about my troops, men and horses. He kept me very busy answering questions.'

There was plenty to ask questions about. At the beginning of August he wrote to his mother in Aix-les-Bains, where she was having a not entirely economy class holiday: 'We have field days all day and every day. Very often ten hours in the saddle at a time – without anything to eat or drink the whole time – and after that I invariably play polo for a couple of hours. However I must say I thrive on the treatment.'

He managed to get off to Goodwood races, and enjoyed a drama at the start of the Goodwood Cup. 'The Prince asked after you as did everyone else. Of course Florizel II [owned by the Prince of Wales] won the Cup in a canter, but at the beginning of the race he shied at the crowd and Watts, who was riding nearby, cut a voluntary' (a charming Victorian phrase for a rider falling off their horse).

Winston welcomed the positives of his new life, but reservations were beginning to surface. 'Four years of healthy and pleasant existence – combined with both responsibility and discipline – can do no harm to me – but rather good. The more I see of soldiering the more I like it – but the more I feel convinced that it is not my métier.'

By the end of the month the long days in the field and the hard games of polo were taking their toll, not so much on the body, but on the mind. 'I find I am getting into a state of mental stagnation,' he writes, 'when even letter writing becomes an effort & when any reading but that of monthly magazines is impossible. It is indeed the result of mental forces called into being by discipline and routine. It is a state of mind into which all or nearly all who soldier – fall.'

He calls it a 'Slough of Despond', no doubt a forerunner of his later 'Black Dog' depressions. He tries to compensate by reading and re-reading his father's speeches, and when his mother then suggests that he use 'The Supply of Army Horses' as a subject for a thesis he reacts strongly. He hears "horse" talked all day, and he feels the absence of the wider education he would have got at Oxford or Cambridge. So he is going to read not monthly magazines but Gibbon's *The History of the Decline and Fall of the Roman Empire* and Lecky's *History of European Morals*. His head is on fire. Stagnate he will not.

In September, the 4th Hussars moved from Aldershot to Hounslow in readiness for the winter break, in which the usual practice for dashing officers was to hone their riding skills, and stiffen their courage in the fox hunting field. Winston's plans were different. He had done more riding in the last six months than in the rest of his life put together. For all his baby face he was hardened. He was secure in the saddle.

He would take his challenge on horseback to an entirely new level and location.

Jennie and Winston: 'We worked together on even terms, more like brother and sister than mother and son'

06

COMING OF AGE IN CUBA, OCTOBER–DECEMBER 1895

"After all Reggie, we are soldiers and should see some fighting. Come out there with me. It might be better than hunting and polo."

Previous page: Spanish forces in Cuba, taken from sketches by WSC sent to *The Daily Graphic*

Where were you, and what were you doing, on your 21st birthday? The answer is usually interesting, and sometimes even significant. With Churchill it was certainly both. He was on horseback, in Cuba, and being shot at for the first time.

How the hell did he get there? And where did the horse come from? And who was shooting at him? The last time we heard from him was in Hounslow!

Everyone thinks they know the outlines of the Churchill story, and virtually everything he ever did, wrote, painted or built has been painstakenly recorded. Yet the list is so endless that we forget to pause and ask for detail. As for what happened in Cuba, you shake your head in disbelief.

This was still 1895, later in the year of his father's death, and Churchill was in distinguished company. He was riding, as he had been for the last week, alongside the 64-year-old General Alvaro Suarez Valdes, the commander of the colonial Spanish forces in Cuba, who was vainly trying to put down the latest incursion of the nationalist rebels. The rebellion was the latest and most successful of a series of revolts which would eventually achieve independence from Spain in December 1898, albeit very much through American assistance. The horse was not Duchess Lily's 'magnificent charger' but a little farm-bred, Arab-type Criollo that could keep up a quite comfortable jog-trot all day and, presumably, was quite steady under fire.

The rebels, mercifully, appear to have been quite bad shots.

If next month your 20-year-old son or brother set off for a riding safari in Cuba you would be quite impressed, would wonder how he had organised all the visas and travel arrangements, and would not expect much back except a few drunken selfies from both in and out of the saddle. What you absolutely would not imagine was the letter penned to 'My dearest Mamma' on 6 December 1895, when Winston finally got back to the safety of the Gran Hotel Inglaterra in the Cuban capital, Havana.

'We attacked the position and advanced across open ground under heavy fire,' he writes.

> The General, a very brave man – in a white and gold uniform on a grey horse – drew a great deal of fire on to us, and I heard enough bullets whistle and hum past to satisfy me for some time to come. He rode right up to within 500 yards of the enemy, and there we waited till the fire of the Spanish infantry drove them from their position. We had great luck in not losing more than we did – but as a rule the rebels shot very high. We stayed by the General all the time and so were in the most dangerous place in the field. The General recommended us for the Red Cross – a Spanish decoration given to Officers – and coming in the train yesterday, by chance I found Marshall Campos and his staff, who told me it would be sent to us in due course.

If you did get such a letter you would probably say, 'He's on something.'

But Churchill wasn't – even if, during his seven-day trek with General Suarez Valdes, he had been introduced to both the rum cocktail and the siesta, presumably in that order.

Professor Hal Klepak, a former Canadian army officer resident in Havana, and lecturer at many universities, is the expert on young Winston's somewhat over-adventurous safari, and author of an unsurpassable and perfectly titled book about it, *Churchill Comes of Age*. Hal knows everything, and can fix anything. Well over a century after Churchill's escapade, he even fixed a smashing little grey horse called Moro for me to ride up the field where the bullets had whizzed by Winston that early morning in 1895.

WSC in November 1895, the only contemporary portrait in Cuba

For me there was no General in white and gold uniform: only a tirelessly helpful farming lady called Odalys riding another grey bareback in white cap, jeans and a blue denim jacket. There was no incoming fire, and the only danger came from the fully sexed Moro making dangerously suggestive squealing noises at Odalys's mare that threatened to put us both into a highly embarrassing position. The ride was only a couple of hours in the afternoon, not the dawn trek through the lifting mist and the 8 a.m. combat. But we were on exactly the same spot in deepest rural Cuba some 250 miles east of Havana, open rolling countryside interspersed with thick, jungly woodland, and the same question kept screaming out of the Caribbean sun – *how on earth did Churchill get here?*

The trivial answer is by boat and train and horseback, because planes had yet to be invented. But how he actually got to be in that embattled Spanish saddle is a tribute to the sheer chutzpah of the small and slender youth who only ten months earlier had been whingeing about the riding school. Certainly he had always possessed an independent, not to say rebellious streak. He had kicked his hated first headmaster's straw hat to pieces, he had written mocking articles for the *Harrovian*, and made a speech from the barriers of the Empire Theatre. He was utterly unfazed in any society, be it with the Prince of Wales or Lance Corporal Hathaway. But he was only turning 21, was the most junior subaltern in his regiment, and had never been west of Central Ireland. What made him think of Cuba?

Not even Professor Klepak, it seems, knows quite why and when the idea of this Caribbean adventure lit up in Churchill's head. But the how is easy.

We can unpick the tangled web of correspondence, contacts and chartered travel that on 20 November 1895 saw him step off the boat in Havana with letters of accreditation in his pocket from the Spanish Minister of War, the head of the British Army, the Director of British Military Intelligence and, just in case the others were not enough, one from Lord Salisbury, the British Prime Minister.

General Navarro's troops, loyal to the
Spanish during the rebellion

The first move was to write to Sir Henry Drummond Wolff,
the British Ambassador in Madrid, doyen of the diplomatic corps,
and most conveniently a former member, along with Lord Randolph,
Arthur Balfour and John Gorst, of the quartet known as 'The
Fourth Party', who had been a radical Conservative splinter group
in the 1880–1885 parliament advocating what they termed 'Tory
Democracy' and as much ridiculing their own party as mercilessly
attacking Gladstone's Liberal government.

Within days of Winston's request, Sir Henry had got a letter
from General Azcarraga, the Minister of War, welcoming Winston
as a 'military observer', and another from the Minister of Foreign
Affairs to Marshall Martinez Campos, the Captain-General of the
Spanish Army and currently in charge of trying to crush the rebels
in Cuba. For Lord Randolph's sake, Sir Henry got Lord Salisbury to
write a letter too.

Churchill's cousin Shane Leslie's damning verdict on the relationship between Randolph and Winston was that 'Few fathers have
done less for their sons. Few sons have done more for their fathers.'
But Lord Randolph's memory not only drove his son's political career;
it also gave access to the highest figures in the land, which Winston
didn't hesitate to exploit whenever possible.

The Spanish side being squared, the English end was hardly more difficult. As was the custom in those days, cavalry officers went on leave from late October to early January, a period which most of them spent hunting. Colonel Brabazon was always going to like the idea of such a different adventure, and Lord Wolseley, the Commander in Chief, had not only been an old friend of Lord Randolph's, but also just happened to be embarking on a biography of the first Duke of Marlborough. Why not do a favour to the old Duke's great-great-great-great-great-great grandson?

It didn't end there. Emboldened perhaps by the impact of his articles in the *Harrovian* and confident, one imagines, of his facility at expressing himself on paper, Winston had contacted the editor of the *Daily Graphic*, for whom his father had written some much-discussed pieces from South Africa in 1892. With apparently little ado he was duly commissioned to deliver five pieces, along with sketches, at five guineas a time. Remember that at current rates that is almost £500 an article – and the boy is still only 20! And just to make sure all will be OK in Cuba, Sir Donald Mackenzie Wallace of the *Times* foreign desk wires their man in Havana to help the young pup as much as possible.

All this was done in little over a month. On 4 October Lady Randolph received a missive that began, 'My dearest Mama, I daresay you will find the content of this letter fairly startling,' and gaily sketched out his travel plans, while neatly failing to explain, except for a passing reference to 'Havana where the Government troops are collecting to go up country', that the main point was to experience being fired at in combat. Winston would sail to New York, take 'a steamer to the W. Indies', and come back via Jamaica, Haiti and New York. The return ticket is £37, he says, and 'the whole thing should cost £90 – which would be within by a good margin what I can afford in two months.' So it would all be hunky-dory – 'a voyage to those delightful islands at the season of the year when their climate is at its best will be very pleasant to me – who has never been on sea more than a few hours at a time. And how much more safe than a cruise [fox hunting] among the fences of the Vale of Aylesbury.'

Lady Randolph's reply is magnificent, both in its acceptance of the life-force that she has mothered – 'you know I am always delighted if you can do anything that interests and amuses you' – and the majesty of its scolding:

> *I won't throw cold water on your little plans, but considering that I provide the funds I think that instead of saying 'I HAVE decided to go' it may have been nicer & perhaps wiser – to have begun by consulting me. But I suppose experience of life will in time teach you that tact is a very essential ingredient of all things.*

'Lady Randolph was a beautiful woman with a vital gaiety that made her the life and soul of any party,' wrote Consuela Vanderbilt, the American heiress who in November 1895 married Randolph's nephew Sunny.

> *She was still, in middle age, the mistress of many hearts, and the Prince of Wales was known to delight in her company. Her grey eyes sparkled with the joy of living, and when, as was often the case, her anecdotes were risqué, it was in her eyes as well as in her words that one could read the implications. She was an accomplished pianist, an intelligent and well-informed reader and an enthusiastic advocate of any novelty.*

Jennie was also a forgiving soul. By the end of the letter to her son she has suggested a friend of hers who will, if needed, get him an introduction to the Governor of Jamaica.

Just 17 days later Winston is writing back triumphantly,

> *The Cuban business is satisfactorily settled. The War Office have given consent & we have this afternoon been to see the head of the Intelligence Department General Chapman, who has furnished us with maps and much information.*
>
> *We are also requested to collect information and statistics on various points, & particularly as to the effects of the new bullet – its penetration and striking power. This invests our mission with an almost official character & cannot fail to help one in future.*

As a sop to his mother's admonishment he adds, 'I shall bring back a great many Havana cigars – some of which can be "laid down" in the cellars of 35 Great Cumberland Place.'

So it was, then, that this rite of passage was undertaken, and in New York Jennie arranged that her son would be under the wing of her Paris amour Bourke Cockran, who proceeded to make a huge impression on Winston, taking him to see both a battleship in the Hudson River and the US Army's equivalent of Sandhurst at West Point, and signed off by booking him a state apartment for the train journey to Tampa Bay for the boat to Cuba.

But in all this – his list of arrangements, and the ride with the Spanish general – Winston Churchill uses 'we', not 'I'. Because there was someone with him: one of the most unsung figures in the Churchill story. It is Reggie Barnes, three years Winston's senior in age, five in army service, and about to be promoted to captain on his return. He is a Devon-born, Winchester-educated vicar's son from Stoke Canon near Exeter, a master horseman who has also spent time in Switzerland. Winston called him 'one of the best friends I shall ever have – perhaps the best'. Without Reggie there would have been no Cuba – and maybe a good deal else less.

Winston and Reggie must have been quite a double act. The best picture of them together is one four years later, on the eve of the Inter-Regimental Polo Championships at Meerut in India. They stand in the back row, side by side on the right edge of the group, little Winston and big Reggie. The smaller man, with his hairless, boyish face, stares out with a challenging glare; the older one's broad shoulders dip in protectively, and above the trim moustache the look is calm but firm. On his own in Cuba, Churchill would have looked too young and too small to be taken seriously, but with Reggie beside him that would not happen. It would be Reggie, as the senior officer, who would be intro-duced first, and who would then bring on, and no doubt sometimes restrain, his brilliant young colleague.

WSC and his 'minder' Reggie Barnes, 'quite a double act'

It had been Winston's idea. Plenty of things usually were. 'After all, Reggie', he had said, 'we are soldiers, and should see some fighting. Come out there with me. It might be better than hunting and polo.' They were cavalrymen, so they did it on horses. It might not be the normal way to celebrate one's 21st birthday, but it would make a great story back in the mess, even if 120 years later Hal Klepak would slightly spoil it by proving conclusively that the actual anniversary had been a couple of days earlier.

In Cuba, Winston and Reggie met up with General Suarez Valdes at Sancti Spiritus, the beautiful 16th-century provincial capital with its colonnaded buildings around the main square all the colours of the paintbox. They were pleased to leave the town early, as smallpox and yellow fever were endemic enough throughout the second half of 1895 to cause a thousand deaths in the area. Churchill called it a 'forsaken place', but when he and Reggie Barnes walked in the dark down the flagstones of the Calle San Rafael Fonda el Correo to report to General Suarez Valdes' headquarters in one of the biscuit-coloured single-storey buildings which still flank the open space of the Plaza Rialto, he was living the dream.

The darkness would be full of unseen presence and noise: the crunch of boot, the stamp of hoof, the bark of order, the jingle of har-ness, the low of oxen, as a 4,000-strong contingent of men, together with horses, carts and provisions, sets off to re-supply bases and seek out the enemy. For the Victorian youth bent on glory this is a heady mix, and Churchill's description in *My Early Life* is vivid enough to have us riding along with him and Reggie, as well as spelling out as clearly as he ever did why he was there in the first place:

> *Behold next morning a distinct sensation in the life of a young officer. It is still dark but the light is paling. We are in what a brilliant though little-known writer has called 'the mysterious temple of the Dawn'. We are on our horses in uniform; our revolvers are loaded. In the dusk and half-light, long files of*

armed and laden men are shuffling off towards the enemy.
He may be very near; perhaps he is waiting for us a mile away.
We cannot tell; we know nothing of the qualities either of our
friends or foes. We have nothing to do with their quarrels.
Except in self-defence, we can take no part in their combats.
But we feel it is a great moment in our lives – in fact one of the
best we have ever experienced. We think that something is going
to happen; we hope devoutly that something will happen; yet
at the same time we do not want to be hurt or killed.

What is it then that we do want? It is that lure of youth –
adventure, and adventure for adventure's sake. You might call
it tomfoolery. To travel thousands of miles with money one
could ill afford, and get up at four in the morning in the hope
of getting into a scrape in the company of perfect strangers, is
certainly hardly a rational proceeding. Yet we know that there
were very few subalterns in the British Army who would not
have given a month's pay to sit in our saddles.

By the time Churchill wrote that he had had to fight his way out
of desperate situations both on the North-West Frontier and in the
Sudan, had several times escaped death by inches in the Boer War and
then, as an officer in the trenches, had been a first-hand witness to
the slaughter on the Western Front. In 1895, however, he and Reggie
were on the glory trail. The 4th Hussars had not seen action since
the Charge of the Light Brigade, when they had finally silenced the
Russian guns, but at the cost of half their men killed or wounded.
The two subalterns had been reared on pictures of manly sacrifice
that felt much more like myth than reality.

'It seemed to my youthful mind,' Churchill wrote as further
explanation of their Cuban foray,

that it must be a thrilling and immense experience to hear the
whistle of bullets all round and to play at hazard from moment
to moment with death and wounds. Moreover, now that I had
assumed professional obligations in the matter, I thought it
might be as well to have a private rehearsal, a secluded trial
trip in order to make sure that the ordeal was one not unsuited
to my temperament.

There is a wry self-mockery in his tone, but that was the mature
Churchill of 1929. Looking back at the relative pantomime of 1895
with the knowledge of horrors to come, he sounds well aware of the
callowness of his younger self.

The young Winston thoroughly approved of what turned out
to be the daily routine: ride from 5 a.m. to 9 a.m.; breakfast; rum
cocktail; a four-hour siesta swinging in a hammock; then another

four hours on the march. When the first actual shot went near him, a day before the so-called Battle of La Reforma, he had been eating a piece of scrawny chicken. Later that afternoon he and Barnes had to get out of the water quickly when the rebels unsportingly interrupted their swimming break, and that night he had a bad fright when a bullet ripped through the hut where he and the others were sleeping in their hammocks. 'I should have been glad to have got out of my hammock and lie on the ground,' he wrote in a passage too good not to repeat here.

> *However, as no one else made a move, I thought it more becoming to stay where I was. I fortified myself by dwelling on the fact that the Spanish officer whose hammock was slung next between me and the enemy's fire was a man of substantial physique, indeed, one might almost have called him fat. I have never been prejudiced against fat men. At any rate I did not begrudge this one his meals. Gradually I dropped asleep.*

In military terms the Battle of La Reforma was no more of a battle than the Subalterns' Cup had been a high-powered horse race, but it clearly made a vivid impression on its most famous participant. 'The firing on both sides became heavy,' he wrote. 'There were sounds about us sometimes like a whistle, and at others like the buzz of an offended hornet. The air was full of whizzings, and the palm trees smitten by the bullets yielded resounding smacks and thuds.' Yet whilst a number of soldiers on either side were injured, and 12 horses were killed, only two actual fatalities seem to have been recorded, and after all the zinging of bullets the two armies upped sticks and marched off in different directions.

But the rebels were getting stronger, and Churchill had already seen and heard enough to realise how tough the outlook was for Spain. 'The more I see of Cuba', he wrote in one of the remarkably percipient and mature 'Letters' he penned for the *Daily Graphic*, 'the more I feel sure that the demand for independence is national and unanimous'. He may have been just 21, but he had the reporter's gift for asking the right questions, hoovering up the answers and then clearly describing the contents. And pith helmets, rum cocktail and siestas notwithstanding, his own daily treks had been tough enough.

It had poured with rain the first morning and several times thereafter. Four hours is a long slog in the saddle, and although the Camino Real (Royal Road) along which they travelled may have been cleared in the king's name, it was nothing more regal than a narrow track through thick jungle. Today most of the jungle has been cleared, but the outlines of the path remain. The day I followed a posse along part of it on my hired horse it didn't rain and the weather wasn't steamy hot, but we jig-jogged along it for long enough to realise that Churchill would have needed all of his toughened cavalryman's backside, and that you would be a sitting duck for any easily concealed sniper.

The day after La Reforma, General Suarez Valdes wanted to get the 15 miles from camp at Jicotea to the train connection at Ciego de Avila, where horses were swapped for trains and gunboats to get the pair back to Havana. They rode it fast across country. It can't have been that different from a Sandhurst paper chase. Altogether they had been in and out of the saddle for seven days.

For the Spanish soldiers, who on that final day marched 'about 21 miles over the worst possible ground, carrying their kit and ammunition, and had in addition been fired on for the best part of four hours', Churchill had nothing but admiration: 'They are fine infantry.' His pencil study of the soldiers gathered round their campfires was among the 16 sketches he did to accompany the vivid, thoughtful and highly commended pieces he wrote for the *Daily Graphic*.

Churchill's ideas of glory were not diminished by this adventure. Being a proven cavalryman had been part of it. The horses he had been given to ride were unlikely to have been more challenging than the two I rode, but being able to handle any horse confidently would have been essential to his acceptance amongst the Spanish officers. For, accustomed to having senior personnel, even generals, as military observers, what must they have thought at the arrival of this boy and his moustachioed minder?

The week of riding through a Cuba beset by civil war had, nevertheless, seen the blithe young man undergo a certain education and maturing. 'There were moments during the last week,' a sobered Winston did admit in his first letter to his mother, 'when I realised how rash we had been in risking our lives – merely in search of adventure. However, it all turned up trumps, and here we are.'

But there were other, equally important matters to be addressed in that same letter to his mother.

'Let me congratulate you on Gold Key's victory,' he wrote, his mother having related how the 'Allotment colt', running in Bob Sherwood's colours, had been the 10-1 winner of a £188 'selling race' at Leicester and cost £180 to buy back.

> I wonder however that you did not let him go after the race. Perhaps he will win a nice stake as a three-year-old. It very often happens that colts who have been – for some reason – very little raced as two-year-olds – win a lot of races the next year. I am thinking of Matchmaker [won 1895 Prince of Wales Stakes] particularly. He was a very useful animal to Sir Frederick Johnstone.

Winston Churchill has just been through the most exciting experience of his life this far, and yet his first comments to his mother are about a winner at Leicester.

He wasn't finished. Towards the end of the letter he contrasts two somewhat disproportionate pieces of good fortune:

> *We went into a town in which every sort of dreadful disease was spreading, and finally if without particular reason I had not changed my position about one yard to the right I should infallibly have been shot. Added to all this I left a fiver to put on 'The Rush' (in the Liverpool Cup) at 8 to I, and it simply romped home. So you see my dear Mamma – there IS a sweet little cherub.*

On 8 December Churchill and Barnes finally took the steamship *Olivette* to Tampa Bay, then entrained for New York from where, on 14 December, they sailed out of the River Hudson on the liner *Etruria* to be home in plenty of time for Christmas. It had been their first taste of long-distance travel. A year later they would be even further afield – and in much more intense riding action.

07

INDIA AWAKENING, 1896

"There is a thrill and a charm of its own in the glittering jingle of the cavalry at the trot, and this deepens into joyous excitement when the same evolutions are performed at a gallop. The stir of the horses, the clank of their equipment, the thrill of their motion, the tossing plumes, the sense of incorporation in a living machine, the suave dignity of the uniform – all combine to make cavalry drill a fine thing in itself."

He was already on his way. For on getting back from Cuba, Churchill had added to his 'Letters' to the *Daily Graphic* a subsequent piece commissioned by the *Saturday Review*. Their publication made him, at 21, an authority on an important foreign policy subject. None other than the Colonial Secretary Joseph Chamberlain wrote that the *Saturday Review* piece was 'the best short account of the problems with which the Spaniards have to deal, & agrees with my own conclusions'.

When a young man is so flagrantly searching for attention, though, some of it is always going to be of the unpleasant kind. As previously described, Churchill was soon to be hit by the Henry Labouchere campaign into the events of the Subalterns' Cup, and he also had to slap down even more lurid allegations from the father of fellow subaltern Allan Bruce, whom Winston and other officers had hounded out of the 4th Hussars for no better reason than that they did not like him. Mr Bruce-Pryce had written to Ian Hogg, brother of Douglas Hogg (later the 1st Viscount Hailsham) that his son knew that whilst at Sandhurst, Churchill had participated in 'acts of gross immorality of the Oscar Wilde type'. A writ was issued within four days, which within a month drew a complete withdrawal and apology and damages of £500 (£50,000 today).

His military career might be surviving such unpleasantness, but by now Winston's long-term aim was already politics and, with his mother networking shamelessly on his behalf, letters such as that from Chamberlain only reinforced that plan. But, as we've just seen with his preoccupation with winners at Leicester, it's still a surprise to realise quite how central horses, and the camaraderie around them, were to it all.

Back then, of course, horses were everywhere. They drove everything bar the water mill and the steam engine. Every house of any pretensions would have one; bigger houses would have a barn-full. Today the 'mews' is synonymous with chichi little houses in Mayfair and other parts of fashionable London tucked away at the back of the great addresses. In the young Churchill's time it was where the stables were located and the carriages kept, ready to come round the front and ferry their masters about town. Today we complain about pollution and exhaust fumes in our cities. At the end of the nineteenth century there was a more natural, but stronger, odour. Just look at the pictures of all those carriages in Piccadilly. To be blunt, there was horse sh** everywhere.

At the beginning of 1896, therefore, at the end of January, when Churchill had been staying at Lord Rothschild's great pile at Tring in Buckinghamshire, the 'very interesting party' of guests had included future premiers and already major players like Herbert Asquith and Arthur Balfour. But Churchill had begun his letter to his mother with the most important fact: 'there is no hunting today.'

When in the 1930s Churchill came to look back, he relished this final flowering of the Victorian age.

*The leading members of Society were in many cases the leading
statesmen in Parliament and also the leading sportsmen on
The Turf. Lord Salisbury was accustomed to scrupulously
avoid calling a Cabinet when there was racing at Newmarket,
and the House of Commons made a practice of adjourning for
the Derby.*

Churchill had the same priorities. Consider, for example, his
panegyric on 'Lord Bill' Beresford, the husband of his aunt Duchess
Lily. 'He seemed to have every quality which could fascinate a young
subaltern,' wrote Winston of his new relative, a winner of many horse
races and holder of the Victoria Cross.

*He was a man of the world acquainted with every aspect of club-
land and society. For long years he had been military secretary
to Lord Dufferin and Lord Lansdowne, successive Viceroys of
India. He was a grand sportsman who had lived his whole life
in companionship with horses. Polo, pig-sticking, pony-racing,
horse-racing, together with shooting big game of every kind,
had played a constant part in his affairs.*

Beresford's younger brother Marcus was the Prince of Wales's
racing manager and like Bill himself had been a dashing rider over
fences. No wonder Winston kept up with what was happening at
Newmarket, Epsom and Aintree.

Imagine the thrill, too, when in March 1896 Captain David
Campbell of the 9th Lancers became the first serving officer to land
the Grand National on The Soarer, a horse he had bought in Ireland
unbroken three years earlier. Seventeen years later, on the Western
Front, the gallant captain was too dashing for his own good when at
Moncel, near Reims, he led the last lance-on-lance cavalry charge
in the history of warfare, and only just lived to tell the tale.

Think of the excitement in the Churchill household, now firmly
if ruinously expensively established at 35a Great Cumberland Place,
when the Prince of Wales led in Persimmon after winning the Derby,
to loyal cheers echoing round and round Epsom Downs. Not only had
Jennie backed Persimmon with good money, but she was now also
entrenched as a leading 'favourite' of the man she nicknamed Tum-
Tum on account of his 48-inch waist. Apparently their speciality was
a 'geisha tea', with her dressed in a fetching kimono.

Even when Churchill wrote to his mother on 1 May about dining
with, amongst others, Lord Wolseley and Joseph Chamberlain, and
having 'quite a long talk on South Africa' with them, it was an equine
metaphor to which he resorted. 'It appears to me that the conspirators
acted like a bad hunter,' he wrote of the fall-out from the abortive
Jameson Raid on Johannesburg at the turn of the year. 'They started
at their ditch at 40,000 miles an hour & then pulled up short on the

Lady Randolph in her furs

edge – with the result that they found themselves carried forward
by their own momentum and in despair made a bound – and fell
– of course.'

The 4th Hussars were winding down their usual activities for
embarkation to India in September, and that May all their horses,
probably including Duchess Lily's 'magnificent charger', were sold
at Tattersalls' famed auction house at Knightsbridge. But first there
had been three major parades to perform. On 14 and 29 April they
were next to the barracks at Hounslow, but that of the 24th was on
Wimbledon Common in front of the Commander in Chief.

'There is a thrill and a charm of its own in the glittering jingle
of the cavalry at the trot,' Churchill wrote in affectionate memory
of these parades,

> *and this deepens into joyous excitement when the same evolu-*
> *tions are performed at a gallop. The stir of the horses, the clank*
> *of their equipment, the thrill of their motion, the tossing plumes,*
> *the sense of incorporation in a living machine, the suave dignity*
> *of the uniform – all combine to make cavalry drill a fine thing*
> *in itself.*

At 10 a.m. on the 11 September 1896, the troopship *Britannia* (not
the same vessel as the Royal Yacht) slipped anchor from Southampton
docks for the three-week voyage to Bombay with Lieutenant Winston
Churchill one of 22 officers aboard, along with two warrant officers,
448 NCOs and other ranks, 28 married women and 45 children who
made up the 4th Hussars' boarding party.

Time, perhaps, before he gallops any further forward, to have
a contemporary picture of the young rider at this time. 'When I first
knew him he was just of age but appeared much younger,' wrote
the American Richard Harding Davis in his 1906 book *Real Soldiers
of Fortune*.

> *He was below medium height, a delicate-looking boy: although*
> *as a matter of fact extremely strong, with blue eyes, many*
> *freckles and hair which threatened to be a decided red but which*
> *now has lost its fierceness. When he spoke it was with a lisp,*
> *which also has changed, and which now appears to be an inten-*
> *tional hesitation. His manner of speaking was nervous, eager,*
> *explosive. He used many gestures, some of which were strongly*
> *reminiscent of his father, of whom he, unlike most English lads,*
> *shy at mentioning a distinguished parent, constantly spoke.*

> *He even copied his father in little tricks of manner. Standing*
> *with hands shoved under the frock coat and one resting on each*
> *hip as though squeezing the waist line; when seated, resting*
> *the elbows on the arms of the chair and nervously locking and*

*unclasping fingers, are tricks common to both. He then had and
still has a most embarrassing habit of asking many questions:
embarrassing, sometimes, because the questions are so frank,
and sometimes because they lay bare the wide expanse of one's
own ignorance.*

Harding Davis was ten years older than Churchill, and in 1896
already a distinguished correspondent who had seen many things
including, in 1890, the botched execution in New York of Harry
Kellum, the first man to die in the electric chair, which ended with so
many volts going through the victim that the place was filled with the
revolting smell of burning flesh. Harding Davis's picture of Winston
has a sweeter scent, but hardly that of the most relaxing passenger
with which to share a three-week sea voyage to the Orient. Good job
his brother officers had the prospect of polo.

The importance which the 21-year-old Winston already ascribed
to horse sport was splendidly captured in an article he contributed
at this time to the *Sandhurst Gazette* under the pseudonym 'Cornet
of the Horse'. 'If there is a game which could prepare a youth for a
soldier's life,' he wrote, 'that game is polo. If there is a more admirable
and elevating sport than fox hunting, it has yet to be discovered.'

To his mother, earlier in the year, he had expanded on his enthusiasm at the prospect of getting stuck into polo, and of course his need
for another substantial subvention.

*I am making extraordinary progress at polo – but I want
very much to buy another pony. I wish you could lend me £200
[£20,000 in today's money!] as I could then buy a really first-
class animal which would always fetch his price. When we sell
the ponies at the end of August he would fetch at least £170, and
the odd thirty I would make good out of the money obtained by
selling the others. You see now I am so near the regimental team
that it might just make the difference of £20 between buying
and selling.*

'Well, goodbye, my darling Mamma,' he signs off, with a truly
remarkable explanation of why he is once again short of funds for his
desired expenditure, 'our finance is indeed involved! If I had not been
so foolish as to pay a lot of the bills I should have the money now.'

Aboard *Britannia*, meanwhile, between the games of whist and
piquet and chess and the amateur debating society, the officers of the
4th Hussars had had a brilliant idea: they pooled their resources and
resolved to ensure they got themselves well mounted for Indian polo,
and in particular for the important Hyderabad tournament, which
was hardly a month away. Once the regiment had docked at Bombay
on 2 October and reached the first rest camp at Poona, 90 miles down
their long, 625-mile trek south-west to their Agram Barracks base just

We won the polo tournament after three hard matches – thus securing a magnificent Silver Cup worth 1,000 rupees. This performance is a record. No English regiment has ever won a first-class match within a month of their arrival from England. The Indian papers express surprise and admiration. I will send you by the next mail some interesting instantaneous photographs – in which you will remark me – fiercely struggling with turbaned warriors.

Polo in this country attracts the interest of the whole community. The telegrams as to the result of a polo match figure as prominently in the newspapers as the European situation. The entire population turns out to watch, betting not infrequently runs into thousands of rupees. Our final match against the Native contingent was witnessed by eight or nine thousand natives, who wildly cheered every goal or stroke made by their countrymen – and were terribly disappointed at the issue.

The pride rings down the years to the accompaniment of the whack of the ball, the snort of the horses, the roar of the crowd and the hot, distinctive scents of the sub-continent. Winston Churchill had plenty to be proud of.

WSC in Bangalore with grooms and
polo ponies

08

THE MADNESS OF THE NORTH-WEST FRONTIER: MALAKAND, INDIA, 1897

"To ride a grey pony along the skirmish line is not a common experience. But I had to play for high stakes and have been lucky to win. I did this three times, on the 18th, 23rd and 30th (September). But no one officially above me noticed it until the third time when poor Jeffreys – a nice man but a bad general – happened to see the white pony. Hence my good fortune. Besides I am so conceited I do not believe the Gods would create so potent a being as myself for so prosaic an ending."

The euphoria of the polo tournament victory had been followed by an elephant ride round Hyderabad with 'Miss Pamela Plowden, the most beautiful girl I have ever seen', but Winston Churchill was already restless. People like her family, he wrote home, are 'like oases in the desert'. 'This is an abominable country to live long in,' he went on in the bitterest of rants: 'Comfort you get – company you miss. I meet few people worth talking to, and there is every temptation to relapse into a purely animal state of existence.'

But of course Churchill didn't – nothing could be further from his nature. At Bangalore the military activity that started with the 6 a.m. parade may have been over by midday, but neither this nor the hours of leisure were often wasted. 'Mr Churchill was a real live one,' recalled the now Sergeant Hallaway who had been kept so busy answering questions at Hounslow.

> *Not stuffy like some of the other officers, if you know what I mean. Easy-going. Always ready for a joke. He hated to see chaps punished. The officers used to inspect the stables every day, but we never knew when they were coming. But Mr Churchill would whisper to me, 'Eleven thirty, sergeant major'.*

> *But the great thing about him was the way he worked. He was busier than half the others put together. I never saw him without pencils sticking out all over him. And once when I went to his bungalow, I could scarcely get in what with books and papers and foolscap all over the place.*

Sergeant Hallaway had put his finger on it. It was Churchill's restless mental as well as physical energy that set him apart. Some might be as keen on the parade ground in the morning, or play as many chukkas in the evening, but no one ever got near what Winston did in the afternoons. While others slept, he embarked on a quite astonishing period of self-education. 'The desire for learning came upon me,' he was to write years later. He read Gibbon's *The History of the Decline and Fall of The Roman Empire* and Thomas Macaulay's *History of England*. That is eight and twelve volumes respectively. He took in Plato, Socrates, Aristotle, Malthus, Adam Smith and Darwin. He went through back numbers of the *Annual Review* and wrote up his own thoughts on world events. In the barracks it may have been Hallaway who was bombarded with questions: in the afternoons Churchill's targets were on a much wider front. There must have been so many books that it's a wonder the sergeant even managed to open the door.

And of course horses, we have always to remember, preoccupied him as much as anything. He may not have saddled his own steed any more often than he cooked his own breakfast, but he knew what should be done and, as in virtually every other subject under the sun, was never shy of lecturing others about it.

Take, for instance, the matter of a racing pony called Lily Of The Valley. As the name suggests, she had been bought by Duchess Lily under the guidance of Uncle Bill Beresford, who wrote an encouraging note including details of his trainer in Bangalore, and was sent out to India in Winston's wake. Jennie Churchill, however, was of a very different mind. 'I want to talk to you very seriously about the racing pony,' she begins (she was still sharing 'geisha teas' with the Prince of Wales, which probably explains some of the passion in her disapproval).

> *It may be dead for all I know, but if it is not I want you to prom-*
> *ise me to sell it. I had a long talk with the Prince at Tulchan & he*
> *begged me to tell you that you ought not to race, only because it*
> *is not a good business in India – they are not square & the best*
> *of reputations get spoiled over it. YOU don't know but everyone*
> *else does that it is next to impossible to race in India and keep*
> *clean hands. It appears that Col. Brab told the Prince that he*
> *wished you hadn't this pony. Sell it & buy polo ponies. I am sure*
> *that you will regret it if you don't.*

Notwithstanding any lingering tarnish from the Subalterns' Cup affair, her son was not having any truck with suggestions that he would succumb to some of the crookedness which was apparently not uncommon in India or, for that matter, anywhere else. 'Of course I shall do what you wish in the matter, and if you insist upon my getting rid of my pony I will sell her,' he begins emolliently – 'but I think you will not mind my pointing out how things really stand.' He then rattles off how it would 'rob my life of one strong interest'; how selling it would involve a substantial loss of money; and how insulting it would be to Uncle Bill. That done, the son completes the argument with another of those paragraphs that leave the reader smiling at his sheer irrepressibility.

> *Considering all things my dearest Mama, you must see how*
> *difficult my position is. If racing in India was confined – as*
> *Col. Brab would have you believe – to a few black legs and other*
> *disreputable persons – of course I would not hesitate – but*
> *when I see ALL those with whom I have to live and many whom*
> *I respect owning ponies – I must confess I don't see you should*
> *expect me to deprive myself of a pleasure which they honourably*
> *and legitimately enjoy – or why you should distrust my ability*
> *to resist the temptation to resort to malpractice.*

He hadn't quite finished. 'You should tell His Royal Highness,' he added pompously a week later, 'if he says anything further about racing in India – that I intend to be just as much an example to the

Indian Turf as he is to the English – as far as fair play goes.' As some-one who has spent his working life in and around the racing scene I only wish Winston's sanctimoniousness had been better repaid by Lily Of The Valley. She did eventually win two little races worth £20 up in Calcutta, but most of her story was of delay and disappointment. In racing it is ever thus.

Then there was his mother's enquiry about a horse she had seen going well out hunting, and the typically financially ambitious reply:

> *Claverhouse – the horse to which you allude – belongs entirely to me. The arrangement I had with Bill Beresford being a most one-sided affair. When the horse broke down I wrote and asked him if he would find a home for it during the summer. He said very kindly that he would and, as he thought the horse was good enough to win a steeplechase, he offered to take it from me on 'racing terms' viz.: He was to pay all expenses and take half the profits. The horse does not appear fast enough to win a chase and he consequently sells it in my interest. It ought to be worth £150 at least. I hope so.*

Money once again – or the lack of it, the abiding worry of these two ever over-extravagant Churchills.

In the spring of 1897 Winston had a rather better and certainly more lovingly detailed idea. 'My Chestnut horse Firefly, a beautiful Arab of delightful manners and extreme breeding, will leave India on 10th prox,' he wrote to his mother at the end of a letter describing a painful crash at polo ('the ground here is so terribly hard that a fall is no joke') that had put him temporarily out of action.

> *I want you to ride him and try and sell him. It ought to be possible to obtain £200 for him, as so fine an Arab is very rare in England. You had better let a man ride him first, as he is a stallion and it is possible that English equine society may lead him astray. Out here he is the quietest beast in the world. Don't let them give him too much corn (four or five pounds a day is quite enough). He should have a little salt mixed in his bran mashes twice a week (just enough to impart a distinctive taste) and should be given plenty of hay. He is a great pet and prefers of all things bread & butter or a biscuit.*

History doesn't relate how much Lady Randolph eventually got for Firefly.

Just as you get fed up, however, with Churchill being vain, high-minded and ambitious, all three of which he undoubtedly was, you have to love him for all the bold and brave and silly things he did – especially on horseback. After a 'somewhat rowdy dinner' he hurt his knee falling off a horse which he and three others were all drunkenly

LORD WILLIAM LESLIE DE LA POER BERESFORD, V.C.
Captain 9th Lancers

'Uncle Bill' Beresford, an archetypal
Victorian hero

trying to ride at the same time at the canter. He competed in every race at a local pony meeting, but although he managed three third places it poured with rain and 'the choc and pink colours secured more mud than glory'. He was lucky to escape with only a badly cut hand when a ricocheting bullet showered him with splinters only a couple of weeks after that heavy fall playing polo:

I am now indeed a cripple. My left hand is closely bound up and useless. My right arm so stiff that I cannot brush my hair. And only with difficulty my teeth. However I am healing beautifully and yesterday I managed to play polo with the reins fastened onto my wrists so that you can see that I am not really very bad.

Churchill's obvious pluck and his utter irrepressibility would have won him a bit of slack from his fellow officers, but they must still have found him an odd one. Because he knew he was different. No one else had the contacts, proven writing ability and political potential that he had.

In the May of 1897 he received a letter from Bourke Cockran. 'I firmly believe you would take a commanding position in public life at the first opportunity which arose,' wrote Cockran, 'and I have always felt that true capacity either makes or finds its opportunity.' At 22 Churchill was already openly talking of standing for parliament. But more immediately he longed for another kind of opportunity. Even on the eve of embarkation for India he had got his mother to badger everyone she knew to have him redeployed to Kitchener's troops in Egypt. The young man who had wanted to prove his courage on his horse now yearned for decorations to endorse it. He had already tasted physical adventure, and he wanted more.

In itself that is not so odd. Every war correspondent, which in the Cuba campaign Churchill had become, wants to cover conflict, and every bold young soldier seeks the chance to test himself in combat. What was exceptional about his next adventure would be how quickly he added the role of combatant to his official one of correspondent, and how much of it would be enacted on horseback.

Winston had first met the splendidly named Sir Bindon Blood, a veteran of every British military campaign since the Zulu Wars, back in the middle of 1896 before the Hussars had embarked for India, at Deepdene, Uncle Bill Beresford's grand, and sadly now demolished, country house in Dorking. Sir Bindon was already a hero of India's frontier wars, and Winston cultivated him to the extent of extracting a promise that on the general's next command a place would be found for Lieutenant Churchill.

A year later, on 26 July 1897, Churchill was back in England on six weeks' home leave from his Indian posting. He briefly interrupted its mainly sybaritic tenor by making his first political speech at Bath, before returning to Deepdene and Uncle Bill for Glorious Goodwood. Hearing at the races that a new campaign to subdue the tribes on the North-West Frontier was being launched in Malakand, with Sir Bindon at its head, the subaltern went to work.

Within minutes he had telegrammed the general reminding him of his promise and, spurning the races, entrained across France and Italy to board ship at Brindisi to make it back to Bangalore by 17 August. Eleven days later, now armed with a message to come up as a war correspondent, largely for the *Daily Telegraph* – his mother had put him in touch – and a commission from Rudyard Kipling's former paper the *Pioneer*, Churchill was at the station with a travel kit, two horses and a servant for the five day, 2,028-mile journey to Nowshera. Another six hours' cart trip across the plain and up through the pass, and Lieutenant Churchill was reporting to the fort at Malakand with the great mountains of the Hindu Kush lowering to the north. The young man in the pith helmet had reached the Mohmand Valley, right up on what is now the Pakistan-Afghanistan border, by the notorious Swat Valley. This was the fabled North-West Frontier. He had come quite a way from Goodwood.

Winston.

A signed portrait of the young warrior

Having left the fort at Malakand, his adventures began with trips out from the new base at Gosam to check the loyalty of the local khans and their tribesmen. If all Churchill had done was to travel up the Jandul Valley with Major Deane and his party on 10 September and describe the salute of the first chieftain it would, for any normal youth, have counted among the best of mountain safaris and most vivid of travel accounts: 'He was a fine-looking man and sat well on a stamping roan stallion,' Winston wrote a couple of months later in his book *The Malakand Field Force*. 'His dress was imposing. A waistcoat of gorgeous crimson, thickly covered with gold lace, displaying flowing sleeves of white linen, buttoned at the wrist. Long, loose, baggy linen trousers, also fastened above the ankle, and curiously pointed shoes clothed his nether limbs…'

But it would not be long before the welcomes were a lot less friendly. At 6 a.m. on the 16th, Churchill was riding out from the makeshift camp ten miles north-west at a place called Inayat Kila, and by the time he returned in the darkness of a soaking thunderstorm his wish for adventure had been granted in the harshest way. His trousers were drenched with another soldier's blood. He had used up a whole revolver magazine to ward off a scimitar-waving tribesman. Another officer was not so lucky, as his body sprawled helpless on the bare rock. 'A tall man in dirty white linen,' Churchill later wrote, 'dropped down upon it with a curved sword. It was a horrible sight.' Next day he would see worse.

Before dawn he was back in the saddle, and at first light was riding out of camp in search of the General and his group, who had not got home overnight. When the mounted band reached the small village of Bilot the General was alive, but nine of his party were not, and another score were badly wounded. Later that day, more than 30 bodies were committed for burial. By his own admission, ever since his initiation in Cuba, Churchill had conceived warfare as a 'glorious game'. All his life he never let his courage or his belief in glory falter – but they had now to be tempered with the cold truths of reality.

As the invading force then advanced up the valleys for the next few weeks, systematically torching crops and villages, we have to imagine the many facets of the extraordinary personality already bubbling under that pith helmet. On the one hand, boastful bluster – 'I only rode about trying to attract attention when things looked a little dangerous', and the reported remark that he was only worried about a wound in the mouth that would stop him talking. On the other, the brave and efficient young soldier Sir Bindon Blood put in charge of a company of non-English speaking Punjabis, of whom the General reported, 'He is working away equal to two ordinary subalterns. He has been mentioned in despatches already, and if he gets the chance will have the VC or the DSO.' Sir Bindon might have been a supportive patron, but should not be dismissed as merely the hard-riding, polo-playing, pig-sticking, tiger-hunting imperialist: he had won a scholarship to Galway University where his father was Professor of Engineering.

But behind the firm, set face, as Churchill sits with such assurance in the saddle, there is a third, more profound side to his character. Well over a century later, what is now officially the Khyber Pakhtunkhwa Tribal Area of Pakistan remains a difficult place to govern. The huge government offensive in Swat Valley against the Taliban in 2009 saw half a million people displaced. In 1897 Winston Churchill's six weeks there were amongst the most intense physical experiences of his life: the long, hard hours in the saddle, the ever-present awareness of a brutally dangerous foe, a bloody baptism in the kill-or-be-killed reality of combat, and all played out against the breathtaking panorama of the mountains and the 'Hampton Court maze' of the valleys beneath. The young man who witnessed all this, who normally allowed his head to rule his heart, also confirms himself as the observer with the special gift of empathy and emotional honesty – who admits to crying when he saw the hacked-to-death body of his friend William Clayton Brown on the stretcher, and allows his pen and his tongue to tell the tale.

When he got back to Bangalore the memories of the village burial at Bilot were still seared on his retina. 'To some the game of war brings prizes, honour, advancement or experience,' he wrote with precocious maturity for a 22-year-old,

> *to some the consciousness of duty well discharged; and to others – spectators perhaps – the pleasure of the play and the knowledge of men and things. But here were those who had drawn the evil numbers – who had lost their all, to gain only a soldier's grave. Looking at those shapeless forms, coffined in a regulation blanket, the pride of race, the pomp of empire, the glory of war appeared but the faint and unsubstantial fabric of a dream: and I could not help realising with Burke: 'What shadows we are, and what shadows we pursue.'*

'I am very gratified to hear that my follies have not been altogether unnoticed,' wrote Churchill to his mother two months after he had returned to safety at Bangalore and been awarded an official Mention in Despatches.

> *To ride a grey pony along the skirmish line is not a common experience. But I had to play for high stakes and have been lucky to win. I did this three times, on the 18th, 23rd and 30th [September]. But no one officially above me noticed it until the third time when poor Jeffreys – a nice man but a bad general – happened to see the white pony. Hence my good fortune. Besides I am so conceited I do not believe the Gods would create so potent a being as myself for so prosaic an ending.*

At the time it was the bravest, if most egotistically foolish piece of riding he ever did. Within a year, his courage would be put to an even sterner equestrian test.

Pathan tribesmen

09

OMDURMAN, SUDAN, 1898

"I was on the hard, crisp desert, my horse at a trot. I had the impression of scattered dervishes running to and fro in all directions."

Previous page: Close combat at Omdurman. Another scene from *Young Winston*

The moment the trumpeter blew 'Right wheel' they knew that this was it. This was the moment their whole cavalry lives had been waiting for. There were 400 of them, lined across in 16 troops, 25-strong, and all of them immediately at the gallop. The 21st Lancers had seen so little combat that cynics said their motto should be 'Thou Shalt Not Kill'. They would now. The enemy were on a ridge to their right and had started shooting. It would take 40 seconds to get the cold steel into them. That's what happened when you sounded 'the Charge'.

This was the Sudan in the soon-to-be-scorching morning of 2 September 1898. It was a dozen miles from Khartoum, where 13 years earlier these same dervish followers of the Mahdi Islamist revolution had killed General Gordon and given Victorian England one of its greatest days of shame. Much blood had already been shed that day. A frontal attack on General Kitchener's army by 15,000 fanatical tribesmen had been brutally shot up by riflemen, Maxim guns, field artillery and a bombardment from the gunboats stationed on the River Nile at the back of the British defensive position. But three times as many dervishes were still somewhere out on the desert plain. The 21st Lancers, whom Churchill had joined in Cairo a month earlier, were meant to be clearing the path for Kitchener to make the two miles to the security of Omdurman, where the White Nile and Blue Nile join for the last 1,000 miles of their journey to the Mediterranean. There seemed to be only a few hundred dervishes out ahead of the Lancers, but the bullets were beginning to count. This thing needed to be done. Yet Churchill had a problem. He was already at the gallop, and needed to get his sword back in its scabbard, and pull the revolver out of its offside holster before reaching the enemy.

The shoulder he had dislocated stepping ashore in Bombay on his first visit to India had never fully mended, and would certainly not sustain the thrusting, slashing intensity of what lay ahead. He was out to the right, the fifteenth of the 16 lieutenants riding in front of their troops and behind their squadron commanders. All those officers were galloping faces set, sword arms outstretched, while behind them rumbled the solid mass of soldiery with those nine-foot-long, steel-tipped lances couched for the charge. It was a medieval scene, the classic '*arme blanche*' of cavalry action. And it was about to be met with its medieval answer.

For as they closed in on what had appeared to be 150 or so riflemen, and perhaps a few hundred scimitar-carrying tribesmen behind them, the eye revealed that the first line was on the lip of a dried river bed in which more than 2,000 warriors were waiting. The Lancers were galloping into a trap, and it was far too late for anything other than increased momentum. 'Charge' is the most emotive word in the military lexicon. It was what all those in the 21st Lancers had always longed for, especially since they had shipped to Egypt two years earlier. It was why they had endured those excruciatingly long training treks under Colonel Martin, who was out ahead of them now, so intent on looking round and encouraging the others that he was to ride in without using either sword or revolver. It was the only acceptable climax to the long, three-week journey up from Cairo, and that dreadful march from Atbara that had cost them 50 horses. Churchill was just a newcomer to their ranks, but he was as addicted to the glory of the charge as anyone. 'After the Frontier,' he wrote a fortnight later, 'I thought – capital – the more the merrier.'

What was about to unfold over the next two minutes would be the culmination of many cavalrymen's lives, and the end for 22 of them. For Churchill it was a new peak of mounted action, but still only a stepping stone on the path he planned. As we have seen, he had never lacked self-belief or pushiness, but his machinations in the year that took him from the North-West Frontier to another grey pony's saddle at Omdurman fairly top the lot.

Moments before impact, the scene as depicted by Edward Matthew Hale

He had hardly returned to Bangalore in November 1897 before he was prodding his mother to solicit a place for him on Kitchener's campaign to subdue the Khalifa and his dervishes in the Sudan. Through winter, spring and into summer he kept up the pressure and finally, despite a very clear refusal from Kitchener himself, managed to pull a flanker by getting the transfer cleared on the highest authority of the Prime Minister, Lord Salisbury.

This is another of the times when you laugh at the lisping little toff. 'I must now go to Egypt,' he grandly writes to his mother within a week of making it back to Bangalore from that 'first blood' trip to Malakand in September, 'and you should endeavour to stimulate the Prince into writing to Kitchener on the subject. He wrote on Villiers' account. Indeed, my life here is not big enough to hold me. I want to be up and doing and cannot bear inaction or routine. Polo has lost half its charm and no longer satisfies me.' If Reggie Barnes knew he was writing home like that he would have clipped him round the ear – perhaps he did. Clearly, though, you couldn't stop Winston sounding off, even if plenty wanted to. The future General Gough met him in the Gunners' Mess in Jumrood on the way back from Malakand, and relates how 'he would lecture all and sundry' from his stance by the fireplace, and the master of the Ooty Hounds (yes, foxhounds – this is colonial India) remembered riding home with this young subaltern who happily confided that he was only using the army as a route for politics.

But for all that, you could not complain about Churchill's commitment to the regiment. When Barnes was away he stepped in as adjutant, and made a big success of it. He organised a concert party when entertainment was needed, with him singing 'Oh, listen to the band' as an opening number – and of course there was the polo. He captained 'the Infants Team' (first year subalterns) in Madras, and had fully established himself in the first team that finished runners-up in the big Meerut tournament to Henry de Beauvoir de Lisle's unbeatable Durham Light Infantry in February 1898. He played up front as number 1, with Albert Savory of Subalterns' Cup fame as the team striker at number 2, the hugely experienced Reggie Hoare at number 3, and Reggie Barnes as the rock at 'Back', number 4. It mattered, and the next year it would matter even more.

The two Reggies and Savory could put up with their lippy number 1, not only because he worked hard on the parade ground and the polo field, but also because of his literary outpourings in the afternoons. Up at the North-West Frontier he had written 12 articles for the *Daily Telegraph*, as well as a number of others for the Indian paper the *Pioneer*. He had already amused his friends with his efforts on an as-yet-unfinished novel, but when he got back from the Frontier he set to work on developing the articles into a single volume, and by New Year's Eve had sent home the manuscript of his first book which, as *The Malakand Field Force*, was published in 1898 to rave reviews and what amounted to a 'herogram' from the Prince of Wales:

I cannot resist writing you a few lines on the success of your book! I have read it with the greatest possible interest and the descriptions and the language are generally excellent. Everybody is reading it and I only hear it spoken of with praise.

Fame is a heady cocktail, as Churchill discovered when he visited Ootacamund (where the Ooty Hunt still continues) for the polo and the races. 'I find myself quite a celebrity,' he wrote smugly to his mother. 'I am paid many compliments, but I always had a good opinion of myself and plenty of ambition, and the book has done nothing to improve the one or stimulate the other.' If it's understandable that Barnes and company could tolerate the bumptious little prodigy in their midst, it is equally easy to appreciate how difficult it must have been for the officers of the 21st Lancers when he was foisted upon them in Cairo on the eve of their departure for the Sudan on 3 August 1898.

For their principal players had been together for ten years, first in India and for the last two in Egypt. They had some formidable horsemen, most notably the five-foot-five Paul Kenna and the six-foot René de Montmorency, a Little-and-Large duo to rival Barnes and Churchill that consistently headed amateur riders' ranks in India. Within three months of arrival in Cairo, Kenna duly topped the Egyptian list. But for all their skills and camaraderie, the 21st Lancers had never seen enemy action, and smarted at the sneering tag of 'Thou Shalt Not Kill'. Kitchener's campaign was their big chance, and no obstacle would prevent them being ready for the Sirdar's (Commander in Chief's) call.

Not even the unexpected Army Order of 1 April 1897 which had converted them from Hussars to Lancers (the soldiers in the ranks of the Lancers now having to learn to charge with nine-foot-long bamboo poles with a steel tip on the end), nor the tortuous three-week combat-ready exercises in the desert, or even the more recent switch from bigger Indian troop horses to smaller, stroppier Syrian stallions. And most certainly not that pushy little know-all Winston Churchill, already notorious for doubling as a press man and army officer, and reputedly very unpopular with the Sirdar because of it. He had only arrived because one of their own Lieutenants had just died of diphtheria, and now they were landed with a cavalry cuckoo at the moment of the most important event in the regiment's history. Despite contrary assurances to Kitchener, Churchill had got commissions to write articles for the *Morning Post,* disguised as letters to his mother which she happily passed on. Imagine what the likes of Kenna and de Montmorency thought of all that.

Time was too short for much antipathy to surface immediately, because within 36 hours of Winston's arrival the entire regiment – that is, 30 officers, 450 other ranks and some 500 horses – was entrained for the 375-mile journey south alongside the Nile to Khizam. There they boarded stern-wheeled paddle steamers for another 400 miles south, broken only by disembarking and riding the horses six miles round the cataracts at Aswan, before boarding more steamers to Wadi Halfa, and then taking another 36 hours on the train down to Atbara.

All this was done in squadrons, and luckily for Churchill he was among friends. The commander, Harry Finn, he knew and liked from Bangalore, and two of the Lieutenants Henry Johnstone and Tom Conolly were not only also recently attached from other regiments but had also been friends of Winston's at Harrow. When the whole regiment got together not everyone was so pally. 'The 21st Lancers are not on the whole a good business,' he then wrote. 'They hate all the number of attached officers, and some of them take little pains to conceal their dislike.'

Away from all these human issues, it's the horses I admire. Think of that grey pony riding steady on the skirmish line in the Mahmund Valley; the relays of struggling little trotters hurrying Churchill up the Malakand pass; the hacks and chargers and polo ponies back in Bangalore – without them all of those great Indian adventures would never have happened. Most of all, imagine the toughness of those little Syrian stallions, carrying the troopers for baking hours in the Sudan, and galloping so fearlessly at Omdurman. When the great war correspondent George Steevens first saw the 21st Lancers ready for the field, they were so hung about with saddle bags, haversacks, water bottles, swords, rifles and other kit that he famously said the troopers 'looked less like horsemen than Christmas trees', and so laden that 'the smallest Syrian had to carry 18 stone; with a heavy man the weight was well over twenty.' As a comparison, nowadays not even the top-weighted horse in the Grand National has to carry more than 12 stone.

Churchill had to get two chargers of his own, paying £40 for one and £35 for the other, and looked on with amusement at the loading process in Cairo.

When I mention that the horses were stallion Arabs, it will easily be realised what a kicking and squealing the stowage of this last item caused. But perseverance overcomes everything, even the vivacity of the little Arab horse, though at times he seems to be actually infected with the fanaticism of the human inhabitants of the land of his birth.

The horses were packed tightly together, and anyone who has ever had a problem with two horses biting each other in a trailer can imagine the carnage with 450 stallions wedged in for hour after hour. No surprise that there were major equine objections when loading started for the final rail leg from Wadi Halfa to Atbara, a 400-mile slog across the Nubian Desert, and that such experts as de Montmorency and Kenna both got badly kicked in the process.

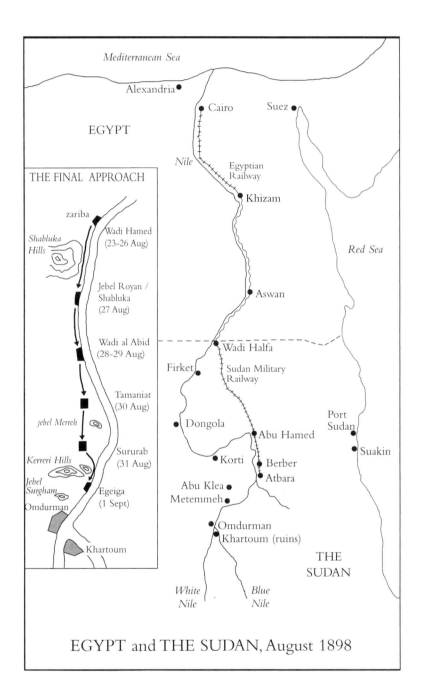

THE FINAL APPROACH

zariba

Shabluka Hills

Wadi Hamed
(23-26 Aug)

Jebel Royan /
Shabluka
(27 Aug)

Wadi al Abid
(28-29 Aug)

Tamaniat
(30 Aug)

Jebel Merreh

Kerreri Hills

Sururab
(31 Aug)

Jebel Surgham

Omdurman

Egeiga
(1 Sept)

Khartoum

Mediterranean Sea

Alexandria

EGYPT

Cairo

Suez

Nile

Egyptian
Railway

Khizam

Red Sea

Aswan

Wadi Halfa

Firket

Sudan Military
Railway

Dongola

Port
Sudan

Abu Hamed

Korti

Berber
Atbara

Suakin

Abu Klea
Metemmeh

Omdurman
Khartoum (ruins)

THE
SUDAN

*White
Nile*

*Blue
Nile*

EGYPT and THE SUDAN, August 1898

The 1,100-mile slog to Omdurman, by rail,
paddle-steamer, rail again and horseback

It took two full weeks to reach Atbara, and yet this was only the start of the most arduous of all the journeys – an eight-day, 240-mile march through the heat down to Kitchener's main holding camp at Wadi Hamed, just 55 miles north of Omdurman. Churchill's campaign nearly expired on the first day when, having to leave later than the others and too close to sunset, he got lost in the darkness without food or water and had to walk towards the rising sun in the morning to slake thirst and find direction from the Nile. 'Jumping off my horse I walked into the flood until it rose above my knees and eagerly to drink its waters as many a thirsty man has done before,' he wrote, 'while the pony, plunging his nose deep into the stream, gulped and gulped and gulped in pleasure and relief as if he could never swallow enough. Water had been found, it remained to discover the column.'

'I like this sort of life,' he had gaily written before this ordeal – 'there is very little trouble or worry but that of the moment, and my philosophy works best in scenes such as these.' But when he finally caught up with the others such optimism had given way to insubordinate anger. 'We are making extraordinary marches of 29 and 30 miles a day, a gross piece of mismanagement and miscalculation by the Sirdar. We kill five or six horses every day. It reveals an amount of folly and wicked waste of public money hardly credible.' Nearly 50 of the regiment's horses had to be destroyed on the march from Atbara to Wadi Hamed, mostly as a result of what Churchill describes as 'a peculiar form of laminitis, caused partly by the hard, hot ground and partly by the sand wearing away the frog of the hoof. The unfortunate horse can hardly walk and doubtless takes every step with agony.'

These, then, were the four-legged heroes who carried Churchill and his fellow cavalrymen at Omdurman and in its arduous prelude. For an image of them you can't do better than the film *Young Winston* made by Richard Attenborough back in 1972. It was actually shot in Morocco but, having myself been out to Sudan and ridden a horse on Churchill's route alongside the Nile as far as the present-day town of Omdurman, which blocks off what would have been the battleground, I can say that the film's landscape approximates as closely to that of the Sudan as its plot does to the story told in *My Early Life*. In particular it gives you an idea of the vast scale and slow movement of things, and the absolute need to have cavalry some five or six miles out ahead to report back on the whereabouts of the enemy. Somewhere on that desert plain were rumoured to be 60,000 dervishes, but riding that Kitchener road you could appreciate that horseback alone is not elevation enough. You need hills in order to get perspective – which is what Churchill did when he climbed up on the first of September and gained a first glimpse of the vast and advancing Mahdi army.

What he saw across the horizon was 'a long black smear' of 50,000 men, gathered under three distinct tribal emblems:

the Green Flag Army, the Black Flag Army, and the White Flag Army. 'It was perhaps the impression of a lifetime,' wrote Churchill of his view from Jebel Surgham, the nearest of the two hills to Omdurman. The three open miles between it and the Kerreri Hills to the north would be the principal field of battle. 'Nor do I expect ever again to see such an awe-inspiring and formidable sight. We estimated their number at not less than 40,000 men, and it is now certain that 60,000 would have been nearer the truth.' This was the message brought back to Kitchener in the film but, instructive as the film sequence is, it cannot get close to the brutality of the conditions and the bravado of the men.

For a start, on 1 September it had poured with rain overnight, and then was swelteringly hot during the day, so that it was a soggy bunch of Lancers who swung into the saddle at 5.30 a.m., and a sweat-soaked and exhausted lot who, bar a few breaks in the day, finally dismounted 12 hours later. Few trips were short – just to get that message back to Kitchener was a ride of six miles, a distance some people these days would consider a full day's exercise. Even stray encounters could be deadly – one cavalry scout was wounded and his horse killed when coming too close to a similar enemy party. But while the sight of the great hosts massed against them was awesome, it was also hugely energising. This was what they were soldiering for.

If the enemy advance continued, the defining conflict would begin within a couple of hours. But while the troops took up defensive lines in a *zariba*, a Sudanese word for 'hedgehog' that here described a semi-circular configuration backed onto the Nile confronting the foe with a thorn-bush-like barrier, what did Churchill and other officers do? They had a good lunch. In his ludicrously well-connected way, Winston was called over by Sir Reginald Wingate, the Director of Military Intelligence, to join his party. 'Everyone was in the highest spirits,' he wrote. 'It was like a race luncheon at the Derby.' It seems an utterly incongruous image, but recall the camaraderie that binds sports teams together – in my racing days, preparations for the Grand National began with champagne in the Turkish Baths at Southport. Here are Churchill's own mid-life reflections on the moment:

> *This kind of war was full of fascinating thrills. It was not like the Great War. Nobody expected to be killed. Here and there in every regiment or battalion, half a dozen, a score, at the worst 30 or 40, would pay the forfeit; but to the great mass of those who took part in the little wars of Britain in those vanished light-hearted days, this was only a sporting element in a splendid game.*

The big game at Omdurman would come not after lunch but before breakfast. At 2 p.m. the Khalifa's warriors inexplicably halted their march, fired their guns in the air and began to make camp,

21st Lancers in battle kit, the lieutenant
depicted is WSC

leaving the likes of Churchill to resume their scouting duties and then pass an uncertain slumber fearing a night attack. But by 5 a.m. they were on their horses, and 20 minutes later were moving out to get news of the enemy. At 6 a.m. Churchill was on the side of the Jebel Surgham hill sending the first of two messages back to HQ of the enemy on the move. 'Talk of Fun!' he wrote with excitement at the memory. 'Where will you beat this! On horseback, at daybreak, within shot of an advancing army, seeing everything and corresponding direct with Headquarters.'

At 6.40 he was disobeying his colonel's order to come back into the *zariba*, and at 6.45 he was a witness to the shock of ancient warriors being smashed up by modern weapons. Six thousand troops of the White Flag Army (the white being actually individual sheets of scripture from the Koran placed on the end of a stick) poured in from the south and east of Jebel Surgham. For the gunboats in the Nile and the artillery in the *zariba* this was an easy target.

> *We were so close as we sat spellbound on our horses that we almost shared their perils. I saw the full blast of Death strike this human wall. Down went their standards by dozens and their men by hundreds. Wide gaps and shapeless heaps appeared in their array. One saw them jumping and turning under the shrapnel blasts; but none turned back.*

Churchill was almost spellbound for too long, and only just galloped back into the *zariba* before the 12,000 men of the Black Flag Army began their attack from the west, and the rains of hell poured out towards them. The result, of course, was just as horrific. The onslaught hitting these medieval warriors totalled 60 cannon, 20 machine guns and 20,000 rifles. G.W. Steevens was inside the *zariba*. 'The torrent swept into them and hurled them down in whole companies,' he wrote for the *Daily Mail*.

> *It was the last day of Mahdism and the greatest. They could never get near and they refused to hold back. By now the ground before us was white with dead men's drapery. Rifles grew red-hot; the soldiers seized them by the slings and dragged them back to the reserve to change for cool ones. It was not a battle but an execution.*

While all this extraordinary onslaught was going on, the Lancers and their horses were sheltering deep down beside the Nile, but once that first battle was won, messengers came round despatching the cavalry to reconnoitre and clear the way for Kitchener to get his troops to Omdurman, leaving the rest of his forces to deal with what was, rightly, guessed to be at least two other 10,000-strong groups of dervishes out on the plain.

The fearsome Hadendoa tribesmen with the heightened hair that won the nickname, the 'Fuzzy Wuzzies'

This was what the 21st Lancers had been waiting for, and Churchill's image of them as they left camp captures their grim and unglamorous purpose. 'We started at a trot,' he wrote in *The River War*,

> two or three patrols galloping out in front, towards the high ground, while the regiment followed in mass – a great square block of ungainly brown figures and little horses, hung all over with water bottles, saddle-bags, picketing gear, tins of bully-beef, all jolting and jangling together; the polish of peace gone; soldiers without grace; but still a regiment of light cavalry in active operation against the enemy.

When the patrols reported back it was to tell of great swathes of defeated troops straggling back towards Omdurman, but one bunch, perhaps a thousand strong, seemed to be lined up to bar the route to the city. It was after 8 a.m., and with the sun up this news was, in the way of these things, relayed by the flashing messages of the heliograph erected on the side of the hill in the face of sniper fire. At precisely 8.30 a.m. the responding heliograph flashed back: 'To Colonel Martin. Annoy them as far as possible on their flank and head them off if possible from Omdurman. Sirdar.'

After it was over, many critics claimed that the charge at Omdurman was as much of a folly as Balaklava, but Colonel Martin's take on the order is fairly understandable. As he led his 400 men and horses across that plain he felt commissioned to clear the field. When he was shot at by what at first looked like a mere 400 riflemen, he correctly swung his force left and into the trot, to see if he could get round his attackers and block their retreat. But he also went into 'Column of Troops' – that is, one after the other, so as to be ready, if he had to, to swing right and charge the quarter-mile distant enemy in one great galloping line of men and horses. Whatever the colonel's thinking, there is no doubt about what his soldiers thought: 'Everyone expected we were going to make a charge,' wrote Churchill. 'That was the one idea that had been in all our minds since we had started from Cairo. Of course there would be a charge.'

As the trumpet sounded and they swung right to face the enemy, Lieutenant René de Montmorency was leading his men five troops along to the left of Churchill, that is a hundred horses across. In the next few minutes René and his racing friend Paul Kenna were both to win the Victoria Cross for their selfless heroics in trying to drag the mutilated body of Thomas Grenfell out of the horrifying frenzy of hacking blades into which the charge had propelled them. De Montmorency's immediate account takes us straight back to what must have been going on for man and mount as this last of the medieval charges got under way. 'Directly we were wheeled into line and charged,' he wrote,

> *a wild feeling of satisfaction and a wish to put sword into an enemy came over me. And as our pace quickened into a fast gallop a wild cheer of excitement and deep satisfaction burst from us, for at last for the first time in the history of the regiment the 21st Lancers were charging in earnest, and the prayer of generation upon generation of 21st Lancers was being granted – and nothing could have stopped us but absolute and complete annihilation.*

Readers should not scoff or sneer. Of course what happens when lance spears infantrymen or scimitar hacks at cavalrymen's heads or horses' hamstrings is brutal and bloody beyond imagining – but so too are all today's infinitely more powerful weapons that literally blow you apart. As far as the 21st Lancers were concerned, they were setting off into history. The Colonel was out front, so intent on looking round and encouraging those behind him that he somehow galloped straight through the 2,000-strong throng of dervishes intended to trap him, unharmed and without drawing either his sword or revolver.

Survivors of the Charge of Omdurman

The shabby, shouting mass behind him included the doctor, the blacksmith, *The Times* correspondent Hubert Howard, and the man destined to be the most famous Briton of them all. We should gallop with them.

'The Dervishes answered us,' continued René de Montmorency,

with fierce hoarse yells of 'Allah il Allah, Khalifa Rasoul Allah' which completely drowned our cheers, and some of them actually bounded joyfully forward to meet us as if victory was already theirs – for they had yet to learn what British Cavalry was. As we closed on them I noticed that my Squadron Leader and Squadron 2nd-in-command were riding with heads down as if riding against a hail storm, and I found myself doing the same – and it was very much like riding against a hail storm as the bullets seemed to hail among us, and there was a continuous 'whizz' 'whizz' 'whizz' and an occasional clink as a bullet hit a sword or lance point.

Just before we hit them I saw straight in front of me a khor [a deep dried riverbed] *with rocks on either side filled with a dense mass of Dervishes packed round three flags, yelling defiance at us, waving their spears and firing their Remingtons, and amidst the smoke and waving arms I could see their upturned faces grinning hate, defiance and satisfaction at us.*

My charger attempted to incline to his left, but I managed to keep him straight, and the next moment he jumped the rocks and I was in the khor amongst them. They were thick as bees, and hundreds of them must have been knocked over by our horses. My charger – a polo pony – behaved magnificently, literally trampling right through them. He only received a slight spear wound and I got through scot-free except for a blow from some blunt weapon across my left arm, and the left flap pocket of my coat cut through, which let out all my food (biscuits) for the day!

This light-hearted reflection is soon drowned out by the sights and sounds of what in two minutes cost his regiment 22 lives, and in all 69 men and 119 horses killed or wounded, the highest proportion of casualties in any of the British engagements on the field. While the Khalifa's forces had been unprepared for the devastation of the gunboats, field batteries and regimented rifle volleys of modern warfare, they had been facing cavalry for centuries. They took the blow of the first impact, and then set about disabling the men and horses at close quarters as they always had. It was not pretty work. 'The sight of our mutilated dead,' confesses de Montmorency, 'made me "see Red" and use very bad language and go for every Dervish I met like a Fury.'

There are countless erudite and illuminating reports of the Charge at Omdurman. Best of all is Terry Brighton's *The Last Charge*, which quotes de Montmorency's recollections and many others. But when we come to Winston Churchill and these most dramatic moments of his riding life, the first and strongest words must come from the man himself. Cram down your hat…

'I propose to describe exactly what happened to me,' he explains in *My Early Life*,

> *what I saw and what I felt. I recalled it to my mind so frequently that the impression is as clear and vivid as it was a quarter of a century ago. The troop I commanded was, when we wheeled into line, the second from the right of the regiment. I was riding a handy, sure-footed, grey Arab polo pony. Before we wheeled and began to gallop, the officers had been marching with drawn swords. On account of my shoulder I had always decided that if I were involved in hand-to-hand fighting, I must use a pistol and not a sword. I had purchased in London a Mauser automatic pistol, then the newest and latest design. I had practised carefully with this during our march and journey up the river. This, then, was the weapon with which I was determined to fight. I had first of all to return my sword into its scabbard, which is not the easiest thing to do at the gallop. I had then to draw my pistol from its wooden holster and bring it to full cock. The dual operation took an appreciable time, and until it was finished, apart from a few glances to my left to see what effect the fire was producing, I did not look up at the general scene.*

There are many alarming sights that can confront you when galloping on horseback. What faced Churchill offered no escape whatever:

> *Then I saw immediately before me, and now only half the length of a polo ground away, the row of crouching blue figures firing frantically, wreathed in white smoke. On my left and right my neighbouring troop leaders made a good line. Immediately behind me was a long dancing row of lances couched for the charge. We were going at a fast but steady gallop. There was too much trampling and rifle fire to hear any bullets. After this glance to the right and left and at my troop, I looked again towards the enemy. The scene appeared to be suddenly transformed. The blue-black men were still firing, but behind them there now came into view a depression like a shallow sunken road. This was crowded and crammed with men rising up from the ground where they had been hidden. Bright flags appeared as if by magic, and I saw arriving from nowhere Emirs on horseback among and around the mass of*

Here come the Lancers, scene as depicted by J Mathews

the enemy. The Dervishes appeared to be ten or twelve deep at the thickest, a great grey mass gleaming with steel, filling the dry watercourse. In the same twinkling of an eye I saw also that our right overlapped our left, that my troop would charge into the air. My subaltern comrade, Wormald of the 7th Hussars, could see the situation too; and we both increased our speed to the very fastest gallop and curved inwards like the horns of the moon. One really had not the time to be frightened or to think of anything else but these particularly necessary actions which I have described. They completely occupied my mind and senses.

Remember, if you are still with him, you have only got one hand on the reins, and falling off is absolutely not an option:

The collision was now very near. I saw immediately before me, not ten yards away, the two blue men who lay in my path. They were perhaps a couple of yards apart. I rode at the interval between them. They both fired. I passed through the smoke conscious that I was unhurt. The trooper immediately behind me was killed at this place and at this moment, whether by these shots or not I do not know. I checked my pony as the ground began to fall beneath his feet. The clever animal dropped like a cat four or five feet down on to the sandy bed of the watercourse, and in this sandy bed I found myself surrounded by what seemed to be dozens of men. They were not thickly packed enough at this point for me to experience any actual collision with them. Whereas Grenfell's troop next but one on my left was brought to a complete standstill and suffered very heavy losses, we seemed to push our way through as one has sometimes seen mounted policemen break up a crowd. In less time than it takes to relate, my pony had scrambled up the other side of the ditch. I looked round.

Somehow he was through, but it was anything but over. And suddenly having a revolver, not a cavalry sword, would make a fateful difference. Dislocating that shoulder had been a godsend.

Once again I was on the hard, crisp desert, my horse at a trot. I had the impression of scattered Dervishes running to and fro in all directions. Straight before me a man threw himself on the ground. The reader must remember that I had been trained as a cavalry soldier to believe that if ever cavalry broke into a mass of infantry, the latter would be at their mercy. My first idea therefore was that the man was terrified. But simultaneously I saw the gleam of his curved sword as he drew it back for a ham-stringing cut. I had room and time enough to turn my pony out of his reach and, leaning over on the offside, I fired two shots into him at about three yards. As I straightened in the saddle, I saw another figure with uplifted sword. I raised my pistol and fired. So close were we that the pistol itself actually struck him. Man and sword disappeared below and behind me.

A few seconds later he avoided a spear thrust by shooting another dervish on the point of throwing – 'how easy it is to kill a man'. He was 'seeing red' just like de Montmorency further up the gully. 'Mr Churchill wanted to charge the enemy again,' remembered Corporal Rix, 'but the Colonel wisely forbade it, instead we formed line, wheeled round to face the enemy's flank, dismounted and opened up a sustained rifle fire. This was more than they could stand, and they finally retreated.'

In just a few minutes what had been one of the most proportionately costly but least important of the day's actions was already over, and Kitchener then marched the bulk of his troops to take possession of Omdurman. Two remaining hosts of dervishes, meanwhile, the Black Flag and Green Flag Armies, both with at least 12,000 men, swung out from behind the hill to threaten the rearguard. Whilst they were being beaten off, Churchill was having to deal with the horrors of war: 'grisly apparitions: horses spouting blood, struggling on three legs, men staggering on foot, men bleeding from terrible wounds, fish-hook spears stuck right through them, arms and faces cut to pieces, bowels protruding, men gasping, collapsing, expiring.'

You can see why that morning was still seared in the memory a quarter of a century later. Indeed, all those extraordinary images would live with him for the rest of his days, and always accompanied by a feeling of gratitude to the four-legged ally who had carried him through: the clever little pony that 'dropped like a cat four or five feet down to the sandy bed of the watercourse' and got him out safe the other side.

It had been, in every sense, the ride of his life.

Colonel Martin, who rode through unscathed without using pistol or sword. An impression by John Charlton

10

POLO CHAMPIONS: MEERUT, INDIA, 1899

"Polo is the prince of games because it combines all the pleasure of hitting a ball, which is the foundation of many amusements, with all the pleasures of riding and horsemanship, and to both of these there is added that intricate loyal team-work which is the essence of football or baseball, and which renders a true combination so vastly superior to the individuals of which it is composed."

Everyone who has ever got involved with a sport dreams of their 'Roy of the Rovers' moment: the time when all the fates conspire and the game, the race, the match comes to a glorious conclusion with you as the star. For Winston Churchill that dream came true one hot Meerut afternoon in Northern India in February 1899. For the first time ever the 4th Hussars polo team had clinched the Inter-Regimental Polo Championship. They had won 4-3 in the final, and he had scored a hat-trick. They don't come much better than that.

So much else of historic importance happened to him later – indeed, was already happening to him then – that we can forget that this was one of the greatest moments of his life. For sport is part of life, and this was unquestionably Churchill's greatest moment in sport. Polo was the biggest thing in his regiment, the Inter-Regimental Polo Championship was the biggest thing in Indian polo, and he was the youngest, smallest and most recent member of the first team.

He went back to India with this goal as a specific priority. In preparation, the team had what amounted to a three-week training camp – first in Madras, and then a fortnight in Jodhpore. Just to make it more heroic, he put his shoulder out on the eve of the tournament, and had to play with his arm strapped to his side. As so often with Winston Spencer Churchill, you couldn't make it up.

Though Winston was always doing so much, much more than the ordinary duties expected of his fellow officers, he kept well up to speed with them. Before he went to the Sudan his commanding officer's citation read: 'A good rider, a very smart cavalry officer and knew my work in the field thoroughly'. When he met up with his 21st Lancers squadron in Atbara a fortnight before Omdurman, Lieutenant Robert Smyth reported, 'Winston Churchill is only 23 and frightfully keen. Started by telling me that he was more interested in men than in horses. He asked to see the men and spoke to them (very well too) and had a great success, in fact they liked him.' The snobbish, egotistical medal-hunter to which he reverts in baser moments is clearly far less than the whole story.

But never has William Blake's famous declaration, 'Energy is the only life', found a better fit. In the few weeks between returning from the Omdurman excitement and his 1 December departure for India and the polo showdown, Churchill's diary encompassed the social, political, journalistic, romantic and sporting to an extent that makes you reach for the whisky bottle. He had a private letter from and then dinner with the Prince of Wales. He cultivated press moguls like Harmsworth (the *Mail*) and Northcliffe (*The Times*) as well as his supportive Borthwick friends at the *Morning Post*. He made political speeches at Rotherhithe, Dover and Southsea. When the pacifist editor of *Concord* magazine wrote in the *Westminster Gazette* that Omdurman was a disgraceful colonial massacre, Churchill leapt into print to reply. If the editor had been there, he wrote, he would have realised that if the spearmen had closed there would have been an even greater slaughter – 'a slaughter in which he himself might have been unfortunately included'.

Everyone now realised his extreme facility with words. One of the great mysteries of the Battle of Omdurman is why and how *The Times*'s correspondent Hubert Howard was, as is generally accepted, galloping with them. Did he carry a sword, a revolver, or just a pocket notebook? We now speak of 'embedded reporters', but this seems ridiculous. But there was no mystery about Howard's view of his fellow scribbler. 'There is Winston,' he had written from Atbara, 'who sits down and in a couple of hours turns out a letter, neat and ready, 100 times better than mine.' Poor Hubert, who was a bright guy and a practising barrister as well as an already experienced war reporter, survived the charge unscathed, but got killed by a 'friendly' shell that same night in Omdurman.

Churchill must have thought – indeed, clearly did – that he was invincible. He had endured the hazards of the Hindu Kush with his trousers soaked in another's blood and not even a bullet through his hat. He had ridden through the dervishes' spears and scimitars without a scratch. He had cheeked Kitchener by getting appointed to the Sudan campaign against the Sirdar's wishes, and then relaying widely acclaimed articles as a war correspondent for a national newspaper. He had already penned one well-reviewed book and was setting up another, to be called *The River War* and, as the writing had already grossed him five times what he had received from the military, once the minor matter of the polo championship had been concluded he was planning to march away.

The ambiguity of his role in the Sudan, despite assurances to the contrary, would catch up with him once he had returned to India. In the columns of the *Army and Navy Gazette*, someone signing himself 'A General Officer' wrote a long disquisition on the question, 'What is the position of Lieut. Spencer Churchill in Her Majesty's Army?' and concluded, 'I am convinced, and I am glad to say that I am not alone in saying this, that this new feature of young subaltern war correspondents has been carried in the case of Lieut. Churchill to the very utmost limit of absurdity.'

When this finally reached Bangalore, it spawned a sweeping and even longer reply, culminating in what we can now recognise, even from a young man only just past 24, as a characteristically Churchillian fanfare: 'I do not wish to further excite the anger of a gallant officer,' he begins with withering sarcasm,

> *nor to show disrespect to his high military rank, but it is necessary in conclusion, whether it be painful or not, to observe that to make personal attacks on individuals, however insignificant they may be, in the publicity of print, and from out of the darkness of anonymity, is conduct equally unworthy of a brave soldier and an honourable man.*

He does not, however, appear to defend himself against the charge!

It is probably time to bring in an informed and erudite witness. G.W. Steevens was the man who had described the 21st Lancers as in 'Christmas tree' order. Like Hubert Howard he would not live to see old age, dying of typhoid in January 1900 during the siege of Ladysmith. But he got to know Winston on the Sudan campaign, and was to voyage back from India with him in March. The *Daily Mail* was running a series of monographs on men with a future, and Steevens' study of Churchill, under the headline 'The Youngest Man In Europe', is so vivid you can almost reach out and touch the human mercury of which it speaks.

'In years he is a boy,' it begins;

> *in temperament he is also a boy; but in intention, in deliberate plan, purpose, adaptation of means to ends he is already a man. In any other generation but this he would be a child. Anyone other than he, being a junior subaltern of Hussars, would be a boisterous, simple, full-hearted, empty-headed boy. But Churchill is a man with ambitions fixed, with the steps towards their attainment clearly defined with a precocious, almost uncanny judgement as to the efficacy of the means to an end.*

It should be stressed that Steevens was anything but a gushing hack. He was the most famous war correspondent of his time, and you can appreciate his perception as he outlines the advantages Churchill took from his aristocratic English background before adding: 'But that inheritance alone would not give him his grip and facility at 24; with us hereditary statesmen and party leaders ripen later. From the American strain he adds to this a keenness, a shrewdness, a half-cynical personal ambition, a natural aptitude for advertisement and, happily, a sense of humour.'

Best of all, G.W. Steevens gives us a full-on portrait clearer than anything on canvas or photo print:

> *His face is square and determined rather than delicate. His body fitter for the platform than the saddle; his colour reddish and sanguine. He looks a boy. As yet, naturally he knows little more than many clever boys, whether of faces or of men. But for all that he has put himself in the directest way of learning. At present he calls himself a Tory Democrat. Tory – the opinions – might change; democrat – the methods – never. For he has the twentieth century in his marrow.*

The reference to a body 'fitter for the platform than the saddle' doesn't square with what we know of Churchill's riding abilities, but is probably best explained by Steevens' description of Colonel

Broadwood, one of the commanders at Omdurman, as 'tall, willowy, long-legged, the perfect horseman's fit for the cavalryman'. Churchill wasn't tall, but he was certainly a keen and practised horseman. And on 7 November, less than a month before returning to India, he was at Kirby Gate, near Melton Mowbray in Leicestershire, for the Quorn Opening Meet. In 1898 this was not just the most important date in the fox hunting year: it was one of the most significant fixtures in the whole sporting calendar.

It's hard to overstate how big a deal fox hunting with packs like the Quorn was at the end of the 19th century. Not only was fox hunting the sporting activity of choice for the ruling elite, but the ultimate in the hunting game was to ride with the Quorn, Cottesmore, Belvoir or Pytchley, the so called 'Shire' packs based in Leicestershire, Rutland and Northamptonshire, and centred on Melton Mowbray. The key to 'the Shires' was their grassy meadows and open, rolling but well-fenced fields, which gave horses the space to gallop but the challenge of jumping, as the hunted fox raced cross-country in search of woodland and an open earth or den. A bold fox, a good scent and an eager pack marshalled by an inspirational huntsman can give runs of five, ten, even fifteen miles to the followers galloping in pursuit of the pack. You don't need a view on the rights or wrongs of fox hunting, banned in Britain since 2005, to comprehend the thrill when the querulous baying of a hound first giving tongue crashes into an urgent chorus from the whole pack, and a 'Holloa!' ringing out across the field tells you that the fox is out in the open and the chase is on.

Even with today's trail hunting, the prospect of grassy fields and beckoning fences can be exciting, but back in 1898 it would have been breathtaking. With fences untrammelled by wire, and fields welcoming entry, only the cautious need tamely follow those seeking the safest route. The bolder could chart their own line, provided they didn't overtake the field master, and on horseback there are few things to equal the challenge of tackling a row of unknown, uncrossed fences, hedges, rails and ditches, most of them with unseen landings – it was the vulpine version of off-piste skiing. My father and grandfather were both MFH (Master of Fox Hounds) and, while such moments didn't happen that often, when they did they were neat spirit to a young man's head, and certainly contributed to my no doubt injudicious career swerve from Oxford graduate to professional jockey.

Winston knew all about the Shires, and it stayed with him. Both his father and his mother had been addicted to hunting in their youth, and the Churchill family had regularly taken Sysonby Lodge in Melton Mowbray for the November-to-March hunting season, stationing more than a dozen horses there for the winter. His cousin Sunny had continued the tradition, and was to become famous for his beautiful grey hunters, and having his grooms bring up fresh horses halfway through the day sporting top hats with green brocade on the side.

The cheetahs trained to hunt antelope

In 1898 Winston did not have long before his return to India, but was clearly making the best of it. 'I have had a very pleasant day's hunting with the Quorn on Sunny's magnificent horses,' he writes to his mother two days after that Monday's opening meet at Kirby Gate, before adding, 'I return to Sysonby tomorrow.' Two days with the Quorn jumping those Leicestershire fences is about as big a thrill as riding can give, and the fun he got out of taking his own line is clearly seen some 30 years later in an appreciation of the cabinet skills of Prime Minister David Lloyd George.

'To use a sporting term,' Winston wrote,

> *he was often hunting in the next field to that through which we were all galloping. Just as we had all made up our minds where to jump the fence, he would exclaim, 'Anyone can see that; but how are we going to get over the canal, or the railway line over there? See, we must make for that bridge or that level-crossing, otherwise we will be hopelessly thrown out. That means a big jump now, and not the easy one you were all thinking about.' I may say he has never hunted with hounds in his life, but had he been born to the part of a nimrod* [the term for a genius of the chase, and someone obsessive about hunting] *instead of to that of a wizard, foxes would have had a bad time.*

Someone whose family loved hunting of all kinds was Pamela Plowden, whom Winston had been distracted by in Hyderabad before the original polo tournament. Her father hunted – but with two trained cheetahs he kept to hunt antelope. But did she love Winston and, more to the point, did he love her? They were always to remain friends, and it was she who later famously said that 'the first time you meet Winston you see all his faults, and the rest of your life you spend discovering his virtues'. Yet she was entitled to be hurt by the jokey and vainglorious end to the letter he sent on the eve of his departure to India, in reply to what had clearly been a long and serious one from her. 'One thing I take exception to in your letter,' he wrote on 28 November: 'Why do you say that

I am incapable of affection? Perish the thought. I love one above all others.' After much playful joshing comes a teasing but revelatory sign-off: 'Who is this that I love? Listen – as the French say – over the page I will tell you.' Overleaf that love is named, 'Yours very sincerely, Winston S. Churchill.' Thirty years later there was a clear recollection of this correspondence in *My Early Life*. 'I began to be much pleased with myself and with the world,' he concludes; 'and in this mood I sailed for India.'

He was still in this mood when he wrote to his mother a month before journeying north to prepare for the polo tournament, albeit with an ever wistful thought for what his life had lacked. 'I work continually at the book' (which would become *The River War*),

and progress slowly but still I think what is written is really good. Let me quote you one sentence – it is about the Mahdi, who was left while still quite young an orphan. 'Solitary trees, if they grow at all, grow strong: and a boy deprived of a father's care often develops, if he escapes the perils of youth, an independence and a vigour of thought which may restore in after life the heavy losses of early days.'

This life is very pleasant and I pass the time quickly and worthily – but I have no right to dally in the pleasant valleys of amusement. What an awful thing it will be if I don't come off. It will break my heart for I have nothing but ambition to cling to. All about myself – as usual.

There were just six weeks before the showdown of the Inter-Regimental Polo Championships in Meerut, and it was time for the sporting party to head north:

Thirty ponies under the charge of a sergeant-major were embarked on a special train for the 1,400-mile journey. Besides their syces they were accompanied by a number of our most trustworthy non-commissioned officers including a farrier-sergeant [head blacksmith], *all under the charge of the sergeant major. The train covered about 200 miles a day, and every evening the ponies were taken out, rested and exercised. Thus they arrived at their destination as fit as when they started.*

'I am playing polo quite well now,' he told his mother. 'Never again shall I be able to do so. Everything will have to go to the war chest.' For Churchill, about to leave the army, this was the last chance to crown what he has described as 'the sustained intensity of purpose with which we threw ourselves into this audacious and colossal undertaking.'

'Polo is the prince of games', he went on,

because it combines all the pleasure of hitting a ball, which is the foundation of many amusements, with all the pleasures of riding and horsemanship, and to both of these there is added that intricate loyal team-work which is the essence of football or baseball, and which renders a true combination so vastly superior to the individuals of which it is composed.

As training camps go, the luxurious home of Sir Pertab Singh, the regent for his young nephew the Maharajah of Jodhpore, some 600 miles north of Bombay, clearly took some beating. Sir Pertab, the most popular and most anglophile of Indian noblemen, was absolutely passionate about playing polo and hosting and instructing British officers in the finer points of the game. Churchill's own account confines itself to polo, but it's worth looking at the more detailed daily schedule outlined three or four years earlier on a similar visit by Hubert Gough, who first met Winston up near Peshawar, and was to encounter him next in South Africa during the relief of Ladysmith. Gough's regiment the 16th Lancers had also been preparing for the Inter-Regimental Championship, so the daily routine was presumably the same.

6 a.m.   Practice ground – one hour of polo practice
7 a.m.   Breakfast
8 a.m.   Camel transport to shoot chinkara [a small Indian gazelle]
12 noon Tiffin – lunch
2 p.m.   Ponies plus shikaree [a local stalker] *for boar hunting*
5 p.m.   Six hard chukkas – against the full Jodphore team

For Gough, incidentally, one sport trumped even polo. 'Of all the sports in India,' he wrote in his memoirs, 'none can compare with pig-sticking.' These days the very term tends to raise a scoffing smile, but in colonial India the duel between a spear carrier on horseback and a wild boar racing over the hazards of the local countryside was one of the greatest challenges for a fearless rider. Gough's preference was certainly shared by Robert Baden-Powell, not only the youngest colonel in the British Army but indeed the host of the Meerut polo tournament. 'There is no doubt,' declared the future founder of the Scout movement, 'that pig-sticking as a sport far transcends any other.'

Under Sir Pertab's watchful eye, meanwhile, preparation for the tournament was being taken, as Winston relates, extremely seriously:

Every evening he and his young kinsmen, two of whom, Hurji and Dokul Singh, were as fine polo players as India has ever produced, with other Jodhpore notables, played us in carefully

*constructed instruction games. Sir Pertab, who loved polo
next to war more than anything in the world, used to stop the
game repeatedly and point out faults or possible improvements
in our play and combination. 'Faster, faster, same like fly,' he
would shout to increase the speed of the game. The Jodhpore
polo ground rises in great clouds of red dust when a game is in
progress. These clouds, carried to leeward on the strong breeze,
introduced a disturbing and somewhat dangerous combination. Turbaned figures emerged at full gallop from the dust
cloud, or the ball whistled out of it unexpectedly. It was difficult
to follow the whole game, and one often had to play to avoid the
dust cloud. The Rajputs were quite used to it, and gradually it
ceased to worry their guests.*

With all this practice, with the seemingly unbeatable Durham
Light Infantry not entered for the tournament, and with the inspirational Sir Pertab barking orders from the touchline like some early
football manager, hopes were rising that the 4th Hussars could gain
their share of polo history. 'Everything smiled,' Churchill subsequently reflected, 'and our chances were good.' Then disaster struck.

'I have had an abominable piece of bad luck,' he wrote to his
mother on 9 February.

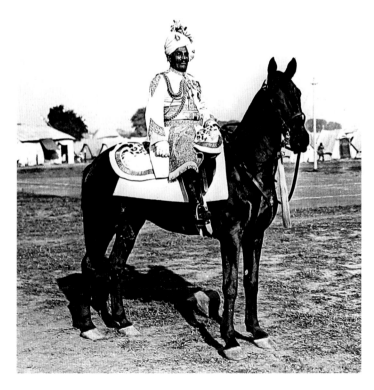

Sir Pertab Singh, the impassioned coach
to the 4th Hussars team

*Last night I fell down the stairs & sprained both my ankles &
dislocated my right shoulder. I am going to struggle down to polo
this afternoon strapped up etc, but I am a shocking cripple and
doubt very much whether I shall be able to play in the tournament.
All these things are minor matters; merely pleasures – I don't
overrate their importance, but I am too young not to feel bitterly
disappointed. The regiment too are very worried as their chances
are weakened. It is better to have bad luck in the little things in life
than in bigger undertakings. I trust the misfortune will propitiate
the gods – offended perhaps at my success & luck elsewhere.*

It wouldn't have mattered much what Churchill did in the first
match, as the 5th Dragoons were routed 16-2. The second round was
a tight 2-1 victory over the 9th Lancers. And so to the final, and the
expected showdown with the 4th Dragoons.

The Hussars decided to nullify the problem of their No. 1's
unfortunate incapacity by using him for what today would be called
the ultimate case of man-marking. 'If the No. 1 was able to occupy the
back,' wrote Churchill, who played in that position with Savory at 2,
Hoare at 3 and Barnes at back, 'ride him out of the game and hamper
him at every turn, then he could serve his side far better than by
overmuch hitting of the ball. We knew that Captain Hargress Lloyd,
afterwards an international player against the United States, was the
back and the most formidable member of the 4th Dragoon Guards.'

What followed must have been, for Hargress Lloyd, about as
exasperating as the ordeal of Brazilian sailor Robert Scheidt when
Ben Ainslie blocked his every move at the back of the fleet to claim
the gold medal on the last day of the Sydney Olympics:

*Up and down the hard, smooth Indian polo ground, where
the ball was very rarely missed and everyone knew where it
should be hit to, we raced and tore. Quite soon we had scored
one goal and our opponents two, and there the struggle hung
in equipoise for some time. I never left the back and, being
excellently mounted, kept him very busy. Suddenly, in the midst
of a confused scrimmage close by the enemy goal, I saw the ball
spin towards me. It was on my near side. I was able to lift the
stick over my head and gave it a feeble forward tap. Through
the goal post it rolled. Two all!*

So, despite his incapacity and his intended man-marking role,
Churchill even managed to score a goal in the final! And not once but
twice more did he manage to effect tap-ins in front of goal, so that,
going into the final seven-minute chukka, the 4th Hussars led 4-3 –
but with one less 'subsidiary' (shots within the flagged area close to
either post), just one more score from the 4th Dragoons would count
the same as an away goal in a Champions League tie. 'You would

not think it was a game at all, but a matter of life and death,' wrote Churchill of that seemingly timeless last chukka. Then came 'one of the most welcome sounds I have ever heard':

> *the bell which ended the match and enabled us to say as we sat streaming and exhausted on our ponies, 'We have won the Inter-Regimental Tournament of 1899.' Prolonged rejoicings, intense inward satisfaction, and nocturnal festivities from which the use of wine was not excluded, celebrated the victory.*

Colonel Baden-Powell presided over the evening. Many toasts had already been drunk when, as he recalled,

> *there suddenly sprang to his feet one of the members of the 4th Hussars team, who said, 'Now gentlemen, you would probably like to hear me address you on the subject of polo.' It was Mr Winston Churchill. Naturally there were cries of, 'No we don't! Sit down!' and so on, but, disregarding all their objections with a genial smile he proceeded to discourse on the subject, and before long all opposition dropped as his honeyed words flowed upon their ears, and in a short time he was hard at it expounding the beauties and the possibilities of this wonderful game. He proceeded to show how it was not merely the finest game in the world, but the most noble and soul-inspiring contest of the whole universe, and having made his point he wound up with a peroration which brought us all cheering to our feet.*

The 4th Hussars team were never to play together again. Within 18 months the South African War would see Albert Savory killed and Reggie Barnes badly wounded. 'Do not grudge these young soldiers their joy and sport,' says Churchill. Let Baden-Powell have the final word on that merry night, and its literally irrepressible hero.

> *When the cheering had died down, one in authority rose and gave voice to the feelings of all when he said: 'Well, that is enough of Winston for this evening' and the orator was taken in hand by some lusty subalterns and placed under an overturned sofa upon which two of the heaviest were then seated, with orders not to allow him out for the rest of the evening.*

> *But very soon afterwards he appeared emerging from beneath the angle of the arm of the sofa, explaining, 'It is no use sitting on me, for I'm India-rubber,' and he popped up serenely and took his place once more in the world and the amusement that was going on around him. I have often remembered the incident on occasions since then, when in politics or elsewhere he has given proof of his statement.*

11

SOUTH AFRICA, 1899–1900

"Suddenly as I ran, I saw a scout. He came from the left, across my front; a tall man, with skull-and-crossbones badge, and on a pale horse. Death in Revelation, but life to me. I shouted to him as he passed: 'Give me a stirrup.'"

Previous page: WSC next to the
wrecked armoured train from which
he had been captured

In the Boer War it was the escape from Pretoria jail that made Churchill 'the most famous man in the Empire', but it was his escape on horseback four months later that saved his life. His guardian angel had already done more shifts than was healthy, and this was definitely overtime. It started with a slipping saddle.

Many of us have been there. The horse is fussing around, you put your foot hurriedly in the stirrup and, as you try to swing aboard, the saddle slips round and you catapult off backwards, leaving the wretched beast to gallop off with the leathers flapping. It's annoying enough at any time. If someone is also trying to shoot you, it's a little close to fatal. That's what happened to Winston Churchill when he was ambushed near Dewetsdorp, 40 miles south-east of Bloemfontein in South Africa, on 22 April 1900.

His three team-mates, and Baden-Powell, were also in South Africa. Baden-Powell had become a household name for holding out at the Siege of Mafeking, and Savory, Barnes and Hoare had all been in the field. Barnes had been badly wounded at Elandslaagte in November 1899, and Albert Savory was to die of wounds after the Battle of Bergendal in August the following year. They had taken the direct route. Needless to say, Churchill's had been a more complicated path.

He had returned to England via Cairo to do more research for *The River War*, and had hardly been back a month before a by-election came up at Oldham and he was invited to be, and accepted as, one of the two Conservative candidates – in the peculiar arrangements of the time, Oldham returned two members, and so Churchill was joined against the Liberals by the trade unionist James Mawdsley. They did well enough, incurring only a 2% swing against the incumbent Conservative government, and Churchill, while unsuccessful, clearly took to campaigning with the enthusiasm almost of a cavalry charge. 'I improve every time, I have hardly repeated myself at all, and at each meeting I am conscious of growing powers and facilities of speech,' he writes to Pamela Plowden, with whom the plot obviously thickens. 'I have had you in my mind more perhaps this week than ever,' he adds, before warming to his memories: 'speech after speech – meeting after meeting – three, even four in one night – intermittent flashes of Heat & Light & enthusiasm – with cold air and the rattle of a carriage in between. A great experience.'

If Pamela had any doubt what sort of an alliance this might be, she would soon find out as Winston decamped to Blenheim to blitz the writing of *The River War*. 'I am still at Blenheim,' he writes to Lady Randolph on 16 August, 'living v. quietly and walking with Pamela in the intervals. I talk of nothing but the book; but it takes my whole energy and strength, and now that the end is so near I am impatient to be done.' A fortnight later he adds that Pamela loves him, and that 'the more I know of her the more she astonishes me.' One imagines the feeling was reciprocated.

Jennie Churchill seems to have been very supportive of her son's romance, as indeed Winston was of his mother's more complicated liaisons. Her pre-eminence amongst the Prince of Wales's amours had been supplanted by Alice Keppel, great-grandmother of Camilla, the wife of the present Prince, and on the rebound Jennie had taken up with George Cornwallis-West, the ultra-sporty 'best-looking man in England', much to his family's disapproval, as he was 20 years her junior. Mind you, the royal relationship seems to have been kept warm enough – in March 1900 she was still addressing the Prince as 'Tres Cher Ami et Monseigneur'.

With *The River War* off to the printers, Churchill had little time for such delicate matters as love: the Boer War was looming. Tension had escalated between the Dutch-origin Boer republics of the Orange Free State and the Transvaal, and the British Empire, which had designs on the lucrative diamond discoveries under Boer control. Much of this territory was worked by British colonial 'Uitlanders', upholding whose rights had been the pretext for the failed 'Jameson Raid' on Johannesburg from December to January 1895–6. The British rejection of the ultimatum from the Transvaal President Kruger on 9 October to remove all troops from his territory led to a declaration of war, immediate strikes in the British-held Natal and Cape Colony, and the besieging of the British garrisons in Kimberley, Mafeking and Ladysmith.

For Churchill it all offered opportunity, and he was about to pull off the sort of journalistic coup that even today would leave scuffling hacks open-mouthed. On 18 September Lord Harmsworth wired him from the *Daily Mail* with an offer to go to South Africa as their war correspondent. Churchill used this to wire his old ally Oliver Borthwick at the *Morning Post*, with his own proposal. The *Morning Post* signed on the line. Churchill would go to South Africa with all expenses covered, and keep copyright on all the work he produced, on the following terms: £1,000 (£100,000 in today's money) for four months' assignment, shore to shore, and £200 (£20,000) a month thereafter. Five grand a week, plus expenses! And he was still two months shy of 25.

On 14 October he sailed on the *Dunnottar Castle*, accompanied by the faithful family valet Thomas Walden, who was having to swap the luxury of Great Cumberland Place for the rigours of campaigning. Also aboard were several newspaper men and the Commander in Chief General Buller and his staff, all of them worried that the Boers would have already capitulated by the time they reached Cape Town. The ship docked on 31 October for them to find that the war was in fact going extremely badly. Mafeking, Kimberley and Ladysmith were all under siege, and it was clear that the fighting and tactical ability of the Boer forces had been gravely underestimated.

Churchill wanted to get out in the field straight away, and by 3 November it was from an iron horse, not a real one, en route with

Pamela Plowden, who loved WSC but turned him down

the *Guardian* journalist J.B. (John Black) Atkins to a boat from East London up to Durban, that he penned his mother: 'I will write to you from Ladysmith. We have had good luck so far, this being the last train to get through from De Aar, and we have gained four days on all the other correspondents. I shall believe I am to be preserved for future things.'

In Durban he received first-hand accounts that this was going to be a much more serious conflict than punishing rebellious tribes on the North-West Frontier or training Maxim guns on the medieval onslaught of dervishes in Sudan. For the hospital ship *Sumatra* was in the harbour, and on it Winston found Reggie Barnes, shot through the thigh on 21 October during the battle at Elandslaagte. 'He told me all about the fighting,' Churchill later remembered, 'and how skilful the Boers were with horse and rifle. He also showed me his leg. No bone was broken, but it was absolutely coal black from hip to toe. The surgeon reassured me that it was only bruising and not mortification [gangrene] as I had feared.'

Within a week Winston too would be at Elandslaagte, not as an act of revenge for his wounded team-mate, but as a prisoner. He had been captured along with 52 others when the Boers ambushed an armoured train and only 21 men and the driver, very gallantly helped by Churchill before he was taken, managed to escape on the uncoupled engine. 'My Lady,' wrote a disconsolate Thomas Walden to Jennie Churchill as only a faithful valet could,

> I am sorry to say Mr Churchill is a prisoner, but I am almost certain he is not wounded. I came down to Maritzburg yesterday to bring all his kit until Mr Winston gets free. I came down in the armoured train with the driver, who is wounded in the head with a shell. He told me all about Mr Winston. He says there is not a braver gentleman in the Army.

The *Morning Post* now had a famous but impotent asset, made even more valuable and vulnerable with the news of him escaping from Pretoria jail on 12 December. The subsequent nine days of frenetic speculation before his resurfacing at Lourenço Marques on the 21st had included 72 hours hidden down a mine shaft, and so it was a mightily relieved correspondent who on the 23rd was carried on the crowd's shoulders to make a speech of thanks from the town hall steps in Durban.

A week later he was both a correspondent and back in the army. For on Christmas Day he got to see the Commander in Chief, Sir Redvers Buller, at his headquarters at Chieveley, about 30 miles south of the beleaguered Ladysmith, and made a great impression. 'He is really a fine fellow,' Sir Redvers wrote to a friend, 'and I must say I admire him greatly. I wish he was leading irregular troops instead of writing for a rotten paper.'

It had, of course, been Churchill's dual role as serving lieutenant and critical war correspondent that had so infuriated Kitchener, and led to the banning of such doubling-up in future. But now, in direct contradiction to the Sirdar's ruling, Sir Redvers handed Winston a commission in the South African Light Horse under Sir Julian 'Bungo' Byng, a regiment that was part of Buller's increasingly frustrated attempts to cross the Tugela River and push north to lift the shame of the siege of Ladysmith. The riding was about to begin – and plenty of it. The *Morning Post* can't have believed their luck. Their man had come cheap at the price.

Within a few days of joining up, Churchill was realising the difficulties both in and out of the saddle. 'Alas, dearest', he wrote to Pamela, 'another retreat'. He was volunteering to ride 18 dangerous miles from Potgieter's Drift (a crossing-point on the River Tugela) back to the HQ at Chieveley, and on 18 January he had to gallop to the scene of a rare success over the Boers, but once there face the brutal cost of war:

> *Here by the rock under which he had fought lay the Field Cornet*
> *of Heilbronn, Mr de Mentz, a grey-haired man of over 60 years,*
> *with firm aquiline features and short beard. The stony face was*
> *grimly calm, but it bore the stamp of unalterable resolve: the look*
> *of a man who had thought it all out, and was quite certain that his*
> *cause was just, and such as a sober citizen might give his life for.*

Durban, December 1899. WSC acknowledges cheers from the crowd after his escape from jail in Pretoria

De Mentz's hand still clutched a letter from his wife. Next to him lay a 17-year-old boy, and further on two British riflemen, 'with their heads smashed like eggshells'. Whatever illusions Winston might have harboured about the wonders of conflict were long gone now. 'Ah, horrible war,' he continued in the same despatch, 'amazing medley of the glorious and the squalid, the pitiful and the sublime, if modern men of light and leading saw your face closer, simple folk would see it hardly ever.'

The problem for any invading army trying to push northwards towards Ladysmith was the twisting Tugela River and the hills surrounding it, which gave ideal cover for the mobile and crack-shot Boer defenders. Four fruitless times General Buller attacked across the Tugela, with Churchill close at hand to witness the cost of failure, most notably the bloody shambles on the flat-topped 1,400-foot mountain that was Spion Kop.

There is no better way of appreciating the challenge the terrain sets than by riding the territory as Churchill had, and as my elder son and I did while researching a book about my grandfather, Churchill's friend and later Cabinet colleague Jack Seely, who also shared the perils of the South African War.

WSC under canvas in South Africa

This end of Natal had, since Churchill's time, remained largely unchanged territory. Behind us as we left camp loomed the height of Mount Alice, from where General Buller had once watched with increasing bafflement as his assorted plans and heliographic signals went disastrously wrong at Spion Kop to the tune of 1,700 casualties, almost ten times those of his opponents. As we looked over at Spion Kop we could envision the geographical reality of that strange statistic that three good shots in January 1899 would have taken out the subsequent saviours of India (Gandhi – there as a stretcher bearer); the Western world (Churchill – war correspondent); and South Africa (Louis Botha – subsequently the first Premier of the Union).

Just in front of us was the serpentine, silently swishing strength of the Tugela River, across it to the right a green plain, and beyond lay the slopes of Vaalkrans where, ten days after Spion Kop, Botha again inspired the Boers to bloody the British nose. It was one thing to cross the Tugela, we could see: quite another to effect an advance through those hills, dense with enemy fighters, to Ladysmith.

Out there on horseback we could appreciate the physicality of what Churchill did, but, looking back in middle age, he makes light of it all. 'Bungo,' he writes, made him assistant adjutant and 'let me go where I liked when the regiment was not actually fighting. Nothing could have suited me better. I stitched my badges of rank to my khaki coat and stuck the long plume of feathers from the tail of the Sakabula bird [the emblem of the South African Light Horse] in my hat and lived from day to day in perfect happiness.' In reality things were much tougher. 'I have had five very dangerous days,' he wrote to Pamela Plowden immediately after the Spion Kop disaster, 'continually under shell and rifle fire, and once the feather in my hat was cut through by a bullet.'

The armoured train and the Pretoria escape made Churchill famous, but it was out around the Tugela on horseback that he proved his worth. In all jobs, and in particular for the newspaper man chasing a story, there are rewards for going the extra mile.

The key to the Spion Kop disaster is its flat and rocky top – 'about as large as Trafalgar Square', wrote Churchill. The British forces took it at night, but the dawn revealed it as an open target for the Boer artillery, with ground too hard to dig adequate defences. As the bombardment continued through the day, and the British commanders looked on in semi-paralysis from the hills on the other side of the Tugela, on the afternoon and night of 24 January 1900 Churchill did what all good journalists should do. He went to find out for himself.

'We passed through the ambulance village,' he wrote next day for the *Morning Post*,

> *and, leaving our horses, climbed up the spur. Streams of wounded met us and obstructed our path. Men were staggering*

*along alone, or supported by comrades, or crawling on hands
and knees, or carried on stretchers. Corpses lay here and there.
Many of the wounds were of a horrible nature. The splinters
and fragments of the shell had torn and mutilated in the most
ghastly manner. I passed about 200 while I was climbing up.*

As a newspaperman he already had more than enough for a
story, but as a soldier he had other duties. He rode back through what
was now fading darkness to report what he had seen to HQ on the
other side of the valley, and then returned to the embattled Colonel
Thorneycroft on the summit with a message that reinforcements
would come in the morning. 'The darkness was intense,' wrote
Churchill of this third ride. 'The track stony and uneven. It was
hopelessly congested with ambulances, stragglers and wounded men.
I soon had to leave my horse, and toiled upwards, finding everywhere
streams of men winding about the almost precipitous sides of the
mountain, and an intermittent crackle of musketry at the top.'

He got his message through, but it was too late. The shattered
Colonel had already ordered withdrawal, and Churchill had to conclude
that it was 'an event which the British people may regard with feelings
of equal pride and sadness. It redounds to the honour of the soldiers,
though not greatly to the generals', although he does add that those
mighty souls were 'trying their best to carry through a task which may
prove to be impossible, and is certainly the hardest ever set to men'.

Finally, on 28 February, a full month of anguish and further
reverses after Spion Kop, the great occasion arrived when the road
was clear to Ladysmith and the siege was lifted. Late in the day
Churchill was invited by General Dundonald to come with him into
the city. 'Never shall I forget that ride,' wrote Churchill with all the
vividness of Longfellow's famous poem about Paul Revere.

*The evening was deliciously cool. My horse was fresh and
strong, for I had changed him at midday. The ground was rough
with many stones, but we cared little for that. Beyond the next
ridge, or the rise beyond that, or around the corner of the hill,
was Ladysmith – the goal of all our hopes and ambitions during
weeks of almost ceaseless fighting. Ladysmith – the centre of the
world's attention, the scene of famous deeds, the cause of mighty
efforts – Ladysmith was within our reach at last.*

*The excitement of the moment was increased by the exhila-
ration of the gallop. Onward wildly, recklessly up and down
hill, over the boulders, through the scrub, Hubert Gough with
his two squadrons, Mackenzie's Natal Carabiniers and the
Imperial Light Horse, were clear of the ridges already. We
turned the shoulder of the hill, and there before us lay the tin
houses and dark trees we had come so far to see.*

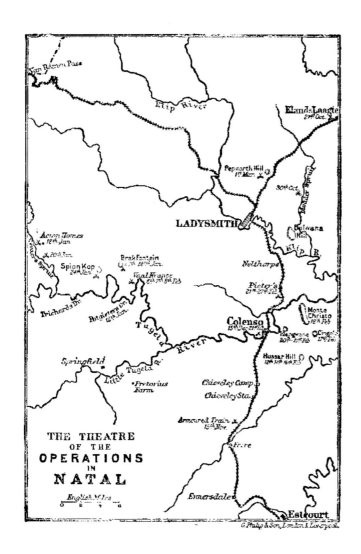

The struggles in Natal before WSC
was involved in the relief of Ladysmith
on 28 February 1900

When they reached the outskirts there was first a challenge, and then exhausted people running out, overcome with relief after 217 starving days of a siege that had transfixed the whole of the British Empire. 'In the half-light they looked ghastly pale and thin,' he wrote of those greeting him. 'A poor white-faced officer waved his helmet to and fro, and laughed foolishly, and the tall, strong, colonial horsemen standing up in their stirrups raised a loud cheer, for then we knew we had reached the Ladysmith picket line.'

Things were only to get better. 'We had begun dinner,' wrote Hubert Gough, who had already reached Sir George White's long-besieged headquarters, 'when the door suddenly opened and Dundonald and Winston Churchill burst in, considerably heated and somewhat excited after their long gallop of about six miles.' As usual,

Churchill, at 25, would be the youngest man in the room. Hubert Gough was only 29, but Ian Hamilton, next to whom Churchill sat, was 20 years his senior, and George White almost 40. At this moment Gough disapproved of Churchill's brashness, while White is supposed to have said, 'I don't like the fellow, but he'll be Prime Minister one day.' Not that any of this quelled Winston's feeling of celebration. 'Never before,' he wrote, 'have I sat in such brave company, nor stood so close to a great event.'

But not everyone at Ladysmith had lived to celebrate. Amongst the victims was George Steevens, the *Daily Mail* writer whom Churchill so much admired, and who had kept spirits up throughout the siege by writing and publishing a witty weekly pamphlet entitled *Ladysmith Lyre*. Readers of the *Morning Post* were reminded that their war correspondent had generosity as well as genius in his pen: 'Sun, stink, and sickness harassed the beleaguered,' wrote Churchill in tribute soon after.

> *The bombardment was perpetual, the relief always delayed; hope again and again deferred. But nothing daunted Steevens, depressed his courage, or curbed his wit. What such a man is worth in gloomy days those may appreciate who have seen the effect of public misfortunes on a modern community.*
>
> *At last he was stricken down by enteric fever* [typhoid]. *When it seemed that the worst was over there came a fatal collapse, and the brightest intellect yet sacrificed by this war perished: nor among all the stubborn garrison of Ladysmith was there a stouter heart or a more enduring spirit.*

Churchill's own bravery in print, and in particular his attitude towards the defeated Boers, did not go down well in more jingoistic circles. In the *Morning Post* he wrote, 'I earnestly hope, expect and urge that a generous and forgiving policy will be followed,' and for the *Natal Witness* he penned a long piece on the same lines, including the ringing invocation: 'Do not act or speak so that it may be said of Natal colonists – "They were brave in battle but they are spiteful in victory."'

By now Churchill's brother Jack was in South Africa too, having arrived to join Winston in the South African Light Horse, only to be shot in the leg on his opening day. Lady Randolph, meanwhile, had, like mother like son, charmed an American millionaire to raise £40,000 (£4 million in today's money) to equip the SS *Maine* as another hospital ship, which was now proudly docked in Durban harbour, where Winston had travelled to meet her, and now Jack became one of his mother's very first patients.

'Winston is being severely criticised for his peaceful telegrams,' Jack wrote to his mother, and when Churchill left Natal for Cape

Town to await press accreditation to General Roberts's staff in
Bloemfontein in the Orange Free State, where future military activity
would be centred, he found much blunt opposition. Luckily the
Governor took an easier line, and clearly Cape Town was not without
its compensations. 'Sir Alfred Milner was far more understanding,'
recalled Churchill, 'and spoke to me with kindliness and compre-
hension. His ADC the Duke of Westminster had organised a pack
of hounds for his chief's diversion and exercise. We hunted jackal
beneath Table Mountain and lunched after a jolly run sitting among
the scrub.'

The idea that the noble Duke had just rustled up some hounds
from nowhere is a bit of an insult to the Cape Hunt, whose hounds
had been 'giving sport' since 1822, when the then Cape Governor
Lord Charles Somerset brought over several couples from the
Beaufort and kennelled them at his hunting lodge, Somerset House,
in the seaside resort of Strand, some 30 miles east of Cape Town.
But it's still a telling image of this high-water mark of the Victorian
age that, wherever the British settled, hunting and racing had to
follow. Naturally Lord Charles had also brought racehorses with him,
and by the time Churchill sat beneath Table Mountain, Kenilworth
Racecourse and 'the Met', South Africa's most famous race, had
already been in existence for 17 years.

Much to his frustration, however, Churchill was not going
anywhere for a while. Up in Bloemfontein Lord Roberts had enough
problems already, and two good reasons for not having the world's
most famous (and most highly paid) war correspondent around.
First, because his ADC was now Kitchener, whose opinion of
Churchill running with the fox and hunting with the hounds was well
established, and secondly because he had himself been offended by
an article of Churchill's slating the feebleness of an army chaplain's
sermon after Spion Kop. Eventually the good offices of Ian Hamilton
caused the General to relent, and any sympathy you may feel
for Churchill will be tempered by his idyllic account of the next
few weeks.

'Equipped by the *Morning Post* on a munificent scale with whatever good horses and transport where necessary,' he remembered in
My Early Life,

> I moved rapidly this way and that from column to column,
> wherever there was a chance of fighting. Riding sometimes
> quite alone across wide stretches of doubtful country, I would
> arrive at the rear-guard of a British column, actually lapped
> about by the enemy in the enormous plains, stay with them for
> three or four days if the General was well disposed, then dart
> back across a landscape charged with silent menace, to keep
> up a continuous stream of letters to my newspaper.

Connections abounded. One of the first commanders he linked with was General Brabazon, his original mentor and colonel in the 4th Hussars. 'Old Bwab' was in charge of the Yeomanry, and attached to him were 'Montmorency's Scouts', who had been raised and commanded by the Omdurman hero René de Montmorency, only for him to be killed on 23 February near Stormberg, with one of his fellow VCs. The Scouts were now commanded by Angus McNeill who, connections again, had done the illustrations for *The River War*. It was McNeill who had promised Churchill some action, and who on 22 April had called him to help cut off some Boer cavalry up ahead.

'So in the interests of the *Morning Post*,' wrote Churchill, 'I got on my horse and we all started – 40 or 50 scouts, McNeill and I, as fast as we could, by hard spurring, make the horses go.' The race was on to make the top of a nearby *kopje* (hill) but, halfway up it, they had to dismount to cut a wire fence and, as they did so, the Boers emerged, rifles cracked out. Desperate re-mounting was required, Churchill's saddle slipped, and there he was, a running if not a sitting duck.

The guardian angel had already diverted bullets in Cuba, India, Sudan, and on many more recent occasions against the Boers. But something very special was needed this time.

> Suddenly as I ran, I saw a scout. He came from the left, across my front; a tall man, with skull-and-crossbones badge, and on a pale horse. Death in Revelation, but life to me. I shouted to him as he passed: 'Give me a stirrup.' To my surprise he stopped at once. 'Yes,' he said shortly. I ran up to him, did not bungle in the business of mounting, and in a moment found myself behind him on the saddle.

It sounds simple, but it's not; especially not with a stamping horse and bullets whistling. The guy in the saddle has to put his left foot forward to free the stirrup, for the other rider to put his own foot in and swing up behind. Churchill would have practised it hundreds of times in the riding school. This was the right place to make perfect.

Yet it was far from over. The horse had already been hit. As the new rider wrapped round his saviour and clutched the mane, he felt his hand moisten – with the horse's blood. The trooper cursed the Boers and bemoaned his animal's fate.

'Never mind,' Churchill told his rescuer, 'you've saved my life.'

'But it's the horse I am worried about,' came the terse response. Trooper Clement Roberts richly deserved his Distinguished Conduct Medal.

My grandfather Jack Seely, meanwhile, had come out to South Africa with his Hampshire Yeomanry by commandeering the SS *Gath* from his uncle's shipping line, and dyeing his grey horse Akbar brown when it was first refused boarding as bad for camouflage. He was that sort of fellow. Now the Hampshire Yeomanry were attached to Sir Leslie Rundle's Eight Brigade, and two days after the escape with Trooper Roberts the illustrious war correspondent came to dinner.

'Winston Churchill shared our very frugal meal the night before the battle,' wrote Jack Seely, 'and expounded to me the plan of attack, the orders for which he had brought me.' By the morning the Boers had got wind of the reinforcements, however, and had vanished during the night, leaving my grandfather to face strangely little opposition. 'Looking up to my right,' he continued,

> I saw a single horseman galloping to the top of the hill which dominated the whole ridge. He waved his hat as he reached the top, and through my telescope I perceived that it was Winston, who, quick to realise the retirement of the enemy, took all risks and rode straight to the objective. Those who had planned the elaborate attack were furious, but of course it was the best thing to do, as it was of no use dawdling when the enemy had gone.

Winston was always keen to position himself as a messenger, and at this strikingly symbolic moment he had excelled himself.

A year on from their 'frugal meal' outside Dewetsdorp, Seely – by now elected as MP for the Isle of Wight – and Churchill were in Westminster together, and a dozen years after that Jack would be Secretary of State for War to Winston's First Lord of the Admiralty. 'Mars and Neptune with 13 medals on their manly chests,' says one description of them sitting side by side at the Speaker's Dinner in Westminster, 'both from Harrow School, and both ex-Tories as chirpy as two boys from a tuck shop.'

For Churchill back in 1900, the last weeks in South Africa were clearly the most enjoyable, and certainly the most mobile, of the whole campaign. For with a four-horse wagon as a base, and with his cousin Sunny Marlborough, and presumably the luckless Walden, as companions, he attached himself to the 11,000 men and 4,000 horses on Ian Hamilton's 400-mile march north from Bloemfontein to Pretoria.

'The wonderful air and climate of South Africa,' he wrote years later of what appears to be the ultimate in horseback safaris,

> the magnificent scale of its landscape, the life of unceasing movement and continuous incident, made an impression on my mind which, even after a quarter of a century, recurs with a sense of freshness and invigoration. Every day we saw new country. Every evening we bivouacked – for there were no tents – by the side of some new stream. We lived on flocks of sheep which we drove with us, and chickens which we hunted round the walls of deserted farms.

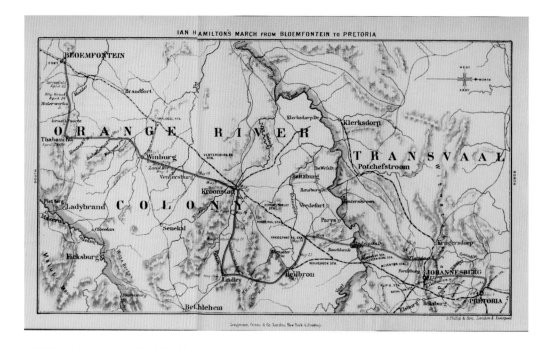

IAN HAMILTON'S MARCH FROM BLOEMFONTEIN TO PRETORIA

'Ian Hamilton's March', the 400-mile trek north from Bloemfontein to Pretoria with WSC, 11,000 men and 4,000 horses

It gets better. 'My wagon had a raised floor of deal boards,' he explains, 'beneath which reposed two feet of the best tinned provisions and alcoholic stimulants which London could supply. We had every comfort, and all day long I scampered about the moving cavalry screens searching in the carelessness of youth for every scrap of adventure, experience or copy.'

There was certainly plenty to write about and, being Churchill, that included several narrow escapes, including cantering almost straight into enemy lines while blinded by smoke, and an incredibly daring bike ride through abandoned but not yet Boer-free Johannesburg to get a message from Hamilton to Lord Roberts's headquarters. If captured, dressed as he was in plain clothes and carrying compromising documents, the only likely conclusion would have been the firing squad. But get through he did, and Winston's belief in his star took him on, before he sailed home, to so conspicuous a piece of bravery at a place called Diamond Hill that Ian Hamilton felt it worthy of the VC.

Yet the happiest moment came when they reached Pretoria. Discovering that the prisoners he had left behind all those months ago (who included Lieutenant Thomas Frankland, who had been on that famous armoured train) were now being held in a different location from the one he had escaped from in December, Churchill set off at the gallop, heedless of who might be defending them. The camp commandant had ordered the prisoners to march to the railway station: they had refused and held him and his aide as hostage, and now their hopes of release hung by a thread.

'Presently, at about half past eight,' recorded Frankland in his subsequent memoir,

two figures in khaki came round the corner, crossed the little brook and galloped towards us. Were they Boers come to order our removal? The advance scouts, perhaps, of a commando to enforce the order! Or were they our friends at last? Yes, thank God! One of the horsemen raised his hat and cheered. There was a wild rush across the enclosure, hoarse discordant yells, and those prisoners tore like madmen to welcome the first of their deliverers. Who should I see on reaching the gate but Churchill, who with his cousin the Duke of Marlborough, had galloped on in front of the army to bring us the good tidings.

In Westminster Hall in November 1954, replying to tributes to his wartime leadership on the occasion of his 80th birthday, the now Sir Winston Churchill reflected, 'It was the nation and the race dwelling all round the globe that had the lion's heart: I had the luck to be called upon to give the roar.' Who is to say that in those last words there was not also a cigar end gleam of the galloping hero cheering the relief of Pretoria jail?

In 45 days Winston Churchill had ridden more than 400 miles. He would never ride as extensively again. During this era of his career, horses had more than once saved his life, and before that they had been life-forming, in shaping one of the greatest lives that was ever lived. From now on they would be strictly a leisure pursuit.

12

HUNTING NEAR AND FAR, 1900–1907

"At the Grand Finale, the Emperor led in person a charge of 30 or 40 squadrons of the centre of the enemy's position. We all galloped along in the greatest glee, and the surging waves of horsemen soon overwhelmed and swept through the rows of venomous-looking little cannons which presumed to confront them."

'I need not say how anxious I am to get back to England,' wrote Churchill to his mother in July 1900 before embarking in Cape Town on the *Dunnottar Castle* for Southampton. 'Politics, Pamela, finances and books all need my attention.' Within seven months he had been a huge success at the first and third, but a dismal failure at the second.

In politics, having fought a much-applauded campaign to become MP for Oldham, he had delivered an acclaimed maiden speech in the House of Commons. On the matter of finance, his book *Ian Hamilton's March* had been published in October, and by Christmas it had sold 9,000 copies. He had embarked on a whirlwind lecture tour in Britain and then in America and Canada, so that on 1 January 1900 he could write from Ottawa, 'I am very proud of the fact that there is not one person who at my age could have earned £10,000 (£1 million 2017) without any capital in the last two years. But sometimes it is very unpleasant work.' But he was not so lucky in love. Back in October, Pamela had turned him down.

She loved him all right. When the news came through about his safe escape in South Africa she had sent a two-word telegram to Lady Randolph: 'Thank God'. 'Pamela is devoted to you,' Jennie had written to her son, 'and if your love has grown as hers – I have no doubt that it is only a question of time for you to marry.' But Pamela also had plenty of suitors, and for a girl of her background the overarching pressure was to marry a man who could give you a house and security of the highest order. For all his brilliance and his extraordinary earning capacity, Winston was renting his cousin Sunny's bachelor flat in Mount Street, Mayfair, and was already as spendthrift as his notoriously extravagant mother. Security was something on which Winston Churchill would never be a decent bet.

No surprise, then, that when Pamela did marry in April 1902, it was to Victor Lord Lytton, master of the vast Tudor Gothic pile that is Knebworth House in Hertfordshire, known now to millions as the setting for films such as *The King's Speech*, and as the venue for vast concerts by megastars of rock. By the time of the marriage, Pamela and Winston's relationship had survived a couple of frissons and returned to a friendship that would last their lifetimes.

It would take a couple more rejections before he found a woman bold and tolerant enough to take him on. First he fell for the American stage star Ethel Barrymore, whose London debut had taken the West End by storm with its catchy opening number:

> *I am Captain Jinks of the Horse Marines,*
> *I often live beyond my means,*
> *I sport young ladies in their teens,*
> *To cut a swell in the army...*

When she returned to London a year later Churchill besieged her, staking out the Savoy every night, but this time the show bombed, the proposal was turned down, and Miss Barrymore escaped to California. A second sally, at the shipping heiress Muriel Wilson, was equally unsuccessful, and the desperate plea, 'Perhaps I shall improve some day', never looked like changing the lovely Muriel's refusal to trade her happy independence for a life in Winston's ever-lengthening shadow.

As Churchill now launched full-tilt into public life there were so many sides to him that following his trajectory is like picking up mercury with your fingers, and it is helpful to concentrate on something simple like horses. Winston's social world now seemed like a permanent film set, and the characters on it extreme to the point of absurdity, albeit at the same time amongst the most powerful figures in the country.

For instance, Warwick Castle, where Winston had proposed – on a punt on the River Avon – was the home of the astonishing Daisy, Countess of Warwick, who was both the socialite former mistress of both the Prince of Wales and of Uncle Bill's brother Lord Charles Beresford, and the philanthropic anti-war socialist who would later blackmail King George V with the threat of revealing his father's letters. It was also the same Warwick Castle where Jennie Churchill had first met George Cornwallis-West, whom, despite the 20-year age gap, she was to marry in July 1900.

By brilliant chance we have Winston Churchill's Badminton Diary for 1901, in that familiar rounded handwriting and what a picture it paints. This is an engagement pad, not a private journal, and its tone is set by the opening advert from East & Co of 7 Curzon Street for 'Carriage Horses – On job for any period.' 'Dine – House of Commons – Conan Doyle', is the kind of routine entry you find in it, as is the word 'Polo', down for Thursday and Friday, 23 and 24 May.

WSC, the young MP

This was a phenomenally busy young man and, when he wasn't engaged in politics or writing, not one to sit around. In three weeks in March he gave seven Boer War lectures as far apart as Chester and Torquay. In the first ten days of April he holidayed from Paris, to Madrid, Seville, Granada, Gibraltar, Cordoba and back again. As for polo: 'I think if I can get two days a week at Hurlingham or Ranelagh' (the former still an exclusive sporting club on the bank of the Thames near Fulham, the latter a little further west at Barnes, and now the Barn Elms estate), he wrote, a shade pompously, to his mother, 'it will provide me with the physical exercise and mental countercurrent that these late hours and continual sitting of the House absolutely require.'

Pompous or not, he was true to his word, with seven 'Polo' entries for May, two days at Windsor after Royal Ascot in June, and on 6 July, having spent the previous three days at the races at Newmarket with his father's and his own financial guru, Sir Ernest Cassel, represented the House of Commons against the Brigade of Guards at Ranelagh. In August and September, Churchill had holiday trips to Scotland, the first of them to the great cliff-top eminence of Dunrobin Castle, the crowning glory of the Duke of Sutherland's 1.3 million acres, where the fellow guests included the young and libidinous Crown Prince of Germany, the son of Kaiser Wilhelm. But, looking at this diary, what really strikes you is the amount of fox hunting.

This was a time when Winston was becoming ever more politically active, as part of a young and rebellious group of Tory MPs, which included my grandfather and Lord Hugh Cecil, from whom they got their 'Hughligans' nickname. Yet in November and December 1901, Churchill fitted in no fewer than 13 days hunting, the first nine of them in the three weeks after the Quorn Opening Meet at Kirby Gate on 4 November. We already know of his declaration in the *Sandhurst Journal* back in 1896 that 'If there is a more admirable and elevating sport than fox hunting, it has yet to be discovered'; while sailing towards Omdurman he had told his mother he was reading R.S. Surtees' *Handley Cross*, with its comic cockney grocer figure of John Jorrocks as a sort of Mr Pickwick of the hunting world. In South Africa a large slice of his *Morning Post* piece on the capture of a Boer wagon convoy had been based on an elaborate hunting metaphor. 'And with this halloa the chase began,' Churchill wrote, 'with apologies to Brooksby,' the legendary hunting correspondent for the *Field* magazine. 'Never in my life have I seen in war so like a fox hunt'. But even at the turn of the century nine days hunting in three weeks was little short of the obsessive.

The Opening Meet of the Quorn at Kirby Gate on 4 November 1901 by Cuthbert Bradley. First published in Vanity Fair

Brooksby Hall, near Melton Mowbray in Leicestershire, was the hunting lodge (big enough to be an agricultural college nowadays) and nom de plume of a classic Victorian figure called Captain Edward Pennell-Elmhirst. If you want to get a flavour of the grip that hunting in Leicestershire held on the imagination, look no further than his 'Brooksby''s report in the *Field* of 7 January 1884:

> *The fences are just what they should be when good turf leads up to their feet – broad, strong, fair and clean. They come easy now, with the last hound flicking through each as we skim the one before, with never a moment for the veriest coward to funk or crane. How long this may last we know not. Suffice it that we conjure nothing better for the seventh – seventeenth heaven.*

With his photographic memory – at Warwick Castle one day he had recited the complete list of the last 50 Derby winners, along with their breeding – Winston could probably rattle off the whole passage verbatim.

Now he plunged into hunting with his usual mixture of enthusiasm and extravagance. He bought himself not one hunter, but four. If you were a landed squire and a man of leisure this might make sense, but if you were an upwardly mobile, socially active, London-based young politician it looked like a case of the eyes being larger than the stomach, not to mention the purse. Quite soon even his cousin Sunny, no stranger to the spending game, was writing reprovingly,

> *Hunting is expensive, and is economical in proportion to the number of days that one hunts. You propose to hunt for 8 weeks, i.e. 50 days. That is, let us say, 20 days hunting. Four horses cost you nearly £400 per annum. The Hunting that you will do will therefore cost you £20 a day [£2,000 in 2017 money]. I consider your arrangements needlessly expensive.*

But let's go with the gallop for, as luck would have it, another Melton devotee, Cuthbert Bradley, did a cartoon for *Vanity Fair* of the 1901 Quorn Hunt Opening Meet at Kirby Gate, which both Sunny and Winston would have attended. The artist's selection of 32 identifiable riders did not include the new recruit, but the list gives an absorbing snapshot at the hunting company Churchill was keeping on that and his other days with the Quorn. Top left of the picture is the Duke of Marlborough, on one of his all-grey stable of hunters. A couple of other leading lights are the sporting Earl of Lonsdale, from whose boxing patronage come the Lonsdale Belts awarded to British champions at every weight, and whose insistence on his coach and livery always being the colour yellow has given that stamp to the AA (Automobile Association), of which he was the founder.

Then there is the MP and archetypal Tory squire Henry Chaplin, who in 1867 had won £120,000 (£12 million at today's value) backing his horse Hermit to win the Derby. (The Marquis of Hastings, meanwhile, who had eloped with Chaplin's fiancée, lost the same amount, and died a year later a ruined man. This world was clearly no place for the parsimonious.) We should not overlook two women in the picture: Daisy, the naughty Countess of Warwick, and the exotically titled Princess Henry of Pless, who had married into European millions of the kind her brother George Cornwallis-West had missed by wedding Lady Randolph.

For Churchill this exotic company was not always uncritical. As his political profile grew, so did his attacks on his own Conservative government on matters like the Army, Free Trade and the use of Chinese labour in South Africa. When, along with my grandfather and several other 'Hughligans', he finally crossed over to the Liberals, the rancour could be personal. There is a report in the Melton Hunting Museum of him having a fall, and the response from the passing enquirer, on being told that he had only hurt his shoulder, is, 'Pity, I hoped he had broken his bloody jaw.'

When not flushed with four horses of his own, Churchill's hunting was largely dependent, as was his Mayfair apartment, on the generosity of his cousin Sunny, who had also heavily subsidised his election expenses, and continued to give him the freedom of Blenheim. He would never hunt with such frequency again – but probably not from a wish to ease his own and the Marlborough finances: rather because of the time involved, and also that, out hunting, Winston could never be more than a mere follower. In every other part of his life he loved to be the leader. The foxes of Leicestershire must have breathed a sigh of relief.

Polo could be fitted in much more easily – and was. Besides his usual games at Ranelagh, Roehampton came on stream with an inaugural tournament on 10 May 1902, and Winston was reported as one of 'the two keenest players at the Roehampton Club', along with David Beatty, the young naval officer who, on the eve of Omdurman, had chucked a bottle of champagne to Winston from his gunboat in the Nile, and who in 1916 would be the admiral commanding the first battlecruiser squadron at the Battle of Jutland.

Of course, Churchill had experienced a gilded introduction to the game during his time in the Army, but not everyone was convinced about polo's benefits. In the early summer of 1902 the feckless ways of some in the military came under censure from a parliamentary report entitled *The Committee on the Education and Training of Young Officers*. Chaired by the Conservative MP Aretas Akers-Douglas, it found that many young officers aimed only 'to see how much polo they can play, and how soon they can get out of uniform', a state of affairs partly down to them apparently having 'nothing to do after luncheon'.

Polo was a favourite diversion for the young MP

Notwithstanding that a lot of this was palpably true, with his own relationship to the sport merely the exception that proved the rule, Churchill went boldly in to bat on young cavalrymen's behalf. 'It is to my mind,' he argued in a letter to the Secretary of State for War, St. John Brodrick, 'a game which develops very strongly qualities of nerve and of judgement quite apart from horsemanship. In all the cavalry regiments I have known, the men who formed the polo team have been the strongest and leading personalities in the regiment, and this because of their character, not because of their proficiency at the game.' He put forward a well-argued case that the problem was the amount of money people were now spending on polo ponies, and that the solution would be to cap how much officers could spend, and press them to train up their own ponies, along the lines perfected by the famous Captain Henry de Beauvoir de Lisle, who had taken his Durham Light Infantry team to three consecutive Inter-Regimental Trophies in 1896–8, beating Churchill's 4th Hussars in the last of them. It was also a thoroughly hypocritical position to take, because Winston was himself now paying over £100 (£10,000 today) a pony, and you will remember that when the 4th Hussars first arrived in India they immediately bought up a whole string of ready-made ponies, and so won that first tournament in Hyderabad.

If all this makes Churchill sound irritatingly privileged, that's because he was. 'Egotistical, bumptious, shallow-minded and reactionary,' was the verdict of Beatrice Webb, the great social reformer (if later deluded in her socialism by a devotion to Stalin) on first meeting him, though she did also acknowledge 'a certain personal magnetism, great pluck and some originality'. Even less forgiving were those on the Conservative side who thought him a traitor for crossing over to the Liberals in 1904, and in June 1905 they pulled off the crowning insult of getting him 'blackballed' at the super-inclusive Hurlingham Club. 'This is almost without precedent in the history of the club,' Winston wrote to the Liberal MP Alexander Murray (usually referred to as the Master of Elibank), 'as polo players are always welcomed. I do not think you and your Liberal friends realise the intense political bitterness which is felt against me on the other side.'

A great example of this came in an addendum to the ultra-Conservative Lord North's hunting diary for the Warwickshire Hounds meet at Broughton Castle, near Banbury, on 6 February 1903, which relates how the hunt followers had got into the Soar Brook, 'where there was a lot of fun especially at the fate of one Winston Churchill, who swam about in it for some time.' The addendum, dated some time after he had switched parties and become a member of the Liberal government, continued: 'If he had been drowned, it would have saved England from the disgrace of having such a SKUNK for a minister.'

Someone who had got to know him rather better – and whose political sympathies also lay somewhat to the left of Tory MPs – was John Black Atkins, the *Guardian* journalist with whom Winston had caught that last train out of Cape Town in 1900. 'I had never before encountered this sort of ambition,' he wrote:

> *unabashed, frankly egotistical, communicating its excitement, and extorting sympathy. He stood alone and confident, and his natural power to be himself had yielded to no man. It was not that he was without the faculty of self-criticism. He could laugh at his dreams of glory, and he had an impish fun: that was what it was in those days, rather than an impish wit.*

You can criticise Churchill for treating politics as just another game like polo, but it was a game he wanted to win for more than egotistical reasons. At its core was his belief in some sort of position in the centre ground: what his father had called 'Tory Democracy', whereby the status quo takes more care of the common man, and in searching for this he liked to listen to older people that he respected.

John Morley, the silver-haired old Liberal who wrote the definitive biography of William Gladstone, was one such. He gave Winston Seebohm Rowntree's seminal book on the plight of the poor in the city of York, *Poverty: A Study of Town Life*. It shocked him deeply, and he wrote a long review castigating the scandal that, despite there being 'all manner of food in plentiful abundance, a large portion of Yorkists endure all the privations which are usually associated with a state of siege'. To others he wrote, 'I see little glory in an Empire which can rule the waves but is unable to flush its sewers,' and as he moved leftwards across the political spectrum he described his ideal of a 'Government of the Middle – the party which shall be free at once from the sordid selfishness and callousness of Toryism on the one hand, and the blind appetites of the Radical masses on the other.'

People could scorn, but they could not discount him, nor deny either his magnetism or his energy. By 1904 he was in Madame Tussauds, and when Wembley Park polo started up in 1905 he could take advantage of special MP's rates in the mornings, as well as his other games at Ranelagh, Roehampton or further afield at Rugby, for which he could stay either at Blenheim, or closer by, with his cousin Ivor Guest at Ashby St Ledgers, the manor house from which in 1605 Robert Catesby and Guy Fawkes planned the Gunpowder Plot.

He certainly had a high opinion of himself, which must at times have been highly aggravating. 'Winston Churchill is undoubtedly exceedingly able,' wrote a fellow guest at Ashby St Ledgers, 'but if you mention a subject to him he instantly must go into oration.' But as the Guardian's J.B. Atkins had noted, there was something winning in his self-confidence – particularly when you appreciated the industry beneath the impishness of the conceit.

In 1902 he had taken on the Herculean task of writing a two-volume biography of his father Lord Randolph, interviewing all the old protagonists and setting up shop wherever he was, sometimes in the unlikeliest of places. 'When we left Dunrobin,' wrote the American author George Smalley, a fellow guest up in Sutherland, 'we found that Winston had reserved a compartment in the railway for himself, and for his big tin case of papers. He shut himself up there, and during that long, long journey, read and wrote as if a Highland railway train were the natural and convenient laboratory in which a literature of the highest order could be distilled.'

Other 'distillation' spots included Sir Ernest Cassel's villa in the Swiss Alps, and most particularly Blenheim Palace, from which he could go and play polo at both Rugby and Oxford's Port Meadow, where he was commended for giving the undergraduate team 'a good gallop' in preparation for the Varsity Match against Cambridge. Needless to say, he did not let his labours go unsung. 'At present,' he wrote to Lord Rosebery as he worked to finish the biography, 'the statesman is in abeyance, and the literary gent and the polo player are to the fore.'

We can get a glimpse of him as he beavers away on a project which was to bring him great acclaim and the enormous sum of £8,000 (no less than £800,000 in today's money). 'He is astonishingly like his father in manners and ways and the whole attitude of his mind,' wrote the author Wilfrid Scawen Blunt, from whom Winston had been seeking information. 'He has just come in from playing polo, a short, sturdy little man with a twinkle in his eye, reminding me especially of the Randolph of twenty years ago.'

The first half of 1906 was both intense and highly charged. The Liberals won a landslide election victory, and at the age of just 31, Churchill found himself in government for the first time in his life, as Under-Secretary of State for the Colonies, and soon tasked with the important role of steering the new Transvaal constitution through the Commons. Nevertheless, on 11 August he went off to gamble and play polo at Deauville, before travelling on around Europe to make it two months away.

'I have been very idle here and very dissipated,' he wrote to his parliamentary secretary Eddie Marsh from Trouville. 'Gambling every night until five in the morning.' His host, aboard a palatial yacht called *Honor*, was a typically larger-than-life protagonist in the Churchill story. Supposedly the son of an American circus performer, but possibly the illegitimate offspring of the hugely landed Baron Hirsch, Baron Maurice De Forest also owned a mighty schloss, Eichhorn Castle, in Moravia, now the Czech Republic. In 1911 he would become a fellow Liberal MP, but not before offering £2,000 for the first Englishman to fly the Channel, and then doubling the money after the Frenchman Louis Bleriot beat 'les Anglais' to it – not to mention himself setting a world motor speed record of 26.6 seconds (84.5 mph) for The Flying Kilometre in Phoenix Park , Dublin in 1903.

Then Churchill moved on to Switzerland to stay with Sir Ernest Cassel. 'I took away £260 from the Deauville Casino' (£26,000 these days), he wrote to his brother Jack, 'some of which I spent in Paris on more beautiful French editions which you might arrange provision-ally on the shelf near the window – & some of which I spent in other directions.' The shelf in question would be in Churchill's new house at 12 Bolton Street, Mayfair; what the 'other directions' may have been we can only feverishly speculate.

If you think Churchill's extra-curricular activities in 1906 sound exotic, however, 1907 saw him shifting up a gear again, with *Strand* magazine commissioning him to write a series of five articles at £150 each, to be subsequently collected into a book for a further £500, on *My African Journey*, while *Punch* would run a series of cartoons featuring 'Winston on Safari'. Imagine the response of today's media to a junior minister making some £120,000, in today's money, out of a procession of assorted safaris and big-game expeditions.

But come the summer there was first a full parliamentary session to negotiate, which inevitably included him and his cousin Ivor being

on the winning side in the Lords v Commons polo match, before
he departed these shores on 17 September, not to return until exactly
four months later. After a look at the French Army's manoeuvres
at Angoulême, he motored with his new friend, the brilliant lawyer
F.E. Smith (later to become the Conservative politician Lord
Birkenhead), all the way down through France and over the French
Alps to Italy via the St Bernard Pass, which must have been quite a
test for a 1907 automobile. From there he drove back up to Moravia to
shoot hare and partridge with Baron Maurice, then down to Syracuse,
where he met up with his secretary Eddie Marsh and boarded
HMS *Venus*, on which they visited Malta, Cyprus and Aden before
docking at Mombasa.

From there it was the Uganda Railway all the way up through
Kenya to Lake Victoria, and then, via steamer, on foot and horseback,
by bicycle and canoe, to the upper reaches of the Nile and sail all the
way down to Khartoum, where there was a miserable Christmas bur-
ying Churchill's devoted servant Tom Scrivings, who had died of food
poisoning. Nine years earlier, Winston had followed another funeral
near Khartoum: that of his fellow soldiers at Omdurman.

WSC (right) on the front of the train which
steamed up from Mombasa

By November, Churchill's boss Lord Elgin, the Colonial
Secretary, was grumbling that the tour was 'originally intended to
be a pure sporting and private expedition, and I really don't know
how it drifted into an official progress', and by 27 December the more
pernickety Sir Francis Hopwood, the permanent Under-Secretary
of State at the Colonial Office, was being far more direct. 'He is most
tiresome to deal with,' Hopwood wrote to Elgin, 'and I fear will give
trouble – as his father did – in any position to which he may be called.
The restless energy, uncontrollable desire for notoriety and the lack
of moral perception make him anxiety indeed.'

Needless to say, none of this appeared to worry Winston. The train had a 'cow-catcher' seat at the front of the engine, on which the British minister and his three colleagues sat and watched 'every animal in the zoo. Zebras, lions, rhinoceros, antelopes of every kind, ostriches, giraffes all on their day – and often five or six different kinds are in sight at the same moment.' He would meet the Governor in Nairobi, and chieftains and district commissioners by long treks out into the bush. One day he was so struck by the scenery around Thika that he cancelled arrangements and rode 28 miles under the distant gaze of Mount Kenya to a little station called Embo, and back again in the morning, his horses having to swim the 60-yard current of the Tana River in the process.

Riding in Kenya remains a captivating experience, and cantering across the vast plains amongst zebra and gazelle and the odd wart hog before camping under the stars still feels as good as it gets, but the political and environmental context nowadays is so utterly different that it is almost impossible to conceive the East Africa Churchill saw.

Nothing contrasts more completely than the attitude to animals. Today's safari hunters just hope to see some: back then they were so plentiful that the idea was not only to see them but also to shoot them. Churchill's hosts constantly apologised for not finding a lion for him to stalk, but on the very first day he records shooting six separate beasts. When on the third day they found a rhino 'in jet-black silhouette, not a 20th-century animal at all, but an odd grim straggler from the Stone Age', his huge sense of wonder did not prevent him undertaking the 'exciting and also anxious work' of shooting it.

Rhinos and most wild game are now so endangered that one can only wince at such an admission, but the purpose here is not to condemn another age but to understand it, and nothing in all Churchill's writing on horseback is more vivid, or indeed revelatory, than his description of a day spent hunting wart hog in the Rift Valley close to Lake Elmenteita, 80 miles north-west of Nairobi.

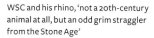

WSC and his rhino, 'not a 20th-century animal at all, but an odd grim straggler from the Stone Age'

Wart hogs today are a non-threatening, rather comical accompaniment to a safari, as they flee away from the riders with their tails as erect as a railway signal, but in Churchill's day the reality appears to have been somewhat different. In contrast to Hubert Gough and Robert Baden-Powell, there is no record of how much pig-sticking Winston had done during his stay in Jodphore before the Meerut Cup Final back in 1899, but now in Kenya he threw himself into the fray. 'Lord Delamere met us at the station with Cape carts, ponies and hog spears,' he wrote,

In Kenya, there was plenty of activity on horseback

> *and we drove off in search of pig over an enormous plain thickly peopled with antelope and gazelle. I cannot pretend to the experience of both countries to compare the merits of pig-sticking in India and in East Africa in respect of the fighting qualities of the animal, nor the ground over which he is pursued. But I should think the most accomplished member of the Meerut Tent Club would admit the courage and ferocity of the African wart-hog, and the extreme roughness of the country, heaped as it is with boulders and pitted with deep ant-bear holes concealed by high grass, make pig-sticking in East Africa a sport which would well deserve his serious and appreciative attention. At present it is in its infancy, and very few even of the officers of the King's African Rifles can boast the proficiency of the Indian expert. But everything in Africa is at its first page; and besides, the wart-hog is at present at any rate, regarded as dangerous vermin who does incredible damage to native plantations and whose destruction – by any method, even the most difficult – is useful as well as exciting.*

The next passage gives a very clear estimation of the equestrian challenge.

> *Our first pig was a fine fellow, who galloped off with his tail straight up in the air, his tusks gleaming mischievously, and afforded a run of nearly three miles before he was killed. The risk of the sport consists in this – that the pig cannot be overtaken and effectively speared except by a horse absolutely at full gallop. The ground is so trappy that one hardly cares to take one's eyes off it for a moment. Yet during at least a hundred yards at a time the whole attention of the rider must be riveted on the pig, within a few yards of whom he is riding, and who may be expected to charge at any second. A fall at such a climax is necessarily very dangerous, as the wart-hog would certainly attack the unhorsed cavalier; yet no one can avoid the chance.*

After the morning's efforts there followed a classic colonial lunch laid out by the end of Lake Elmenteita, and then we return to our man and his evocation of the sheer physicality of this African ride. You may have many images of Churchill over the years as schoolboy, speechmaker, sportsman, cabinet minister, war hero and writer; add to it this:

> *It was late in the afternoon when we started back to the train, which lay eight miles off in a siding. On the way we fell in with a most fierce and monstrous pig, who led us a merry dance through bush and grass and boulder. As he emerged into a patch of comparatively smooth, open ground I made up my mind to spear him, urged my pony to her top speed and was just considering how best to do the deed when, without the slightest provocation, or, at any rate, before he had been even pricked, the pig turned sharp round and sprang at me as if he were a leopard. Luckily my spear got in the way, and with a solid jar which made my arm stiff for a week, drove deep into his head and neck before it broke, so that he was glad to sheer off with 18 inches of it sticking in him.*

Winston's cavalry duties might be long over, but his readiness for combat on horseback was clearly undimmed.

WSC, already a star in the Commons

13

A WORLD RIDING TO WAR, 1907–1918

"It is such fun riding with you and
when you are able to gallop really fast
over beautiful turf it will be a great
joy to us both."

A world riding to war. The world was changing, and fast. Nineteen hundred and six had seen Churchill playing polo and gambling at Deauville during two months holidaying on the continent, which also included expensive shopping in Paris and a stay in Sir Ernest Cassel's chalet in Switzerland. But while he liked to play, he liked the bigger games best. Not many people's idea of being 'very idle and dissipated' includes writing a detailed 35-page resumé of the Transvaal issues for the King, as Churchill did on the luxury yacht *Honor*. Nor spending five days watching German military manoeuvres in Silesia, for which he had procured an official invitation from Kaiser Wilhelm in his role as an honoured and interested member of the government.

'Every night a full dress banquet with the Emperor or Empress in attendance, bed not before midnight,' he wrote,

> *only to be aroused at three or four o'clock in the morning to join the special train which conveyed us to the particular point of the battlefield where the situation could be studied.*

> *Here, as the first light paled the Eastern sky, we mounted our horses and, each accompanied by an officer of the German General Staff, set off wherever we liked to go. After 10 or 12 hours of riding about and watching the operations, we gathered again for the special train at some new point and got back to Breslau in time to dress for the next banquet followed by an Imperial tattoo, another brief interlude of sleep and another four o'clock in the morning departure.*

The chance to have one of the greatest writers in history as our mounted witness while a 50,000-strong force of troops, horses and artillery parade passed by is too good to miss:

> *The infantry, regiment by regiment, in line of battalion quarter columns, reminded one more of great Atlantic rollers than human formations. Clouds of cavalry, avalanches of field guns and – at that time a novelty – squadrons of motor cars (private and military) completed the array.*

> *Like others in the handful of British officers , who in various capacities were watching the operations, I had carried away from the South African veldt a very lively and modern sense of what rifle bullets could do. On the effects of the fire of a large number of guns we could only use our imagination.*

Military tactics had, of course been Churchill's fascination ever since his earliest memory of playing with his set of toy soldiers under the aura of his great military ancestor at Blenheim. It was his reading on the subject which had engaged him intellectually at Sandhurst, and his knowledge and swift perception of military moves that had already given his despatches from so many fronts their uniquely authoritative flavour.

Scenes from Silesia would not disappoint. 'Some inkling of the truth about modern fire had already begun to circulate in the German Army,' Churchill reported, his eye ever open for absurdity.

> *As we advanced over the rolling downs, accompanying an attack delivered by at least 100 guns, and of thousands of happily harmless rifles, I noticed signs of impatience among the German officers with whom I rode. A Princess, who in full uniform was leading her regiment, was in the easy assurance of Royal privilege indignantly outspoken. 'What folly!' she exclaimed. 'It is madness. The Generals should all be dismissed.'*

This was not a film set. This was actually happening with the most powerful military force the world at that stage had ever seen. It was indeed folly for cavalry to gallop straight at gunfire on a thoroughly modern scale. Even the Princess could see that.

The Kaiser and his guest at the German manoeuvres

Churchill was watching the nature of warfare change before his eyes – from the primarily cavalry-based, at times almost sportive, combat he had grown up with and loved, to the industrialised, mechanised slaughter of modern war, which would be unleashed by Germany on the Western Front in less than a decade. It's worth closing your eyes and taking a deep breath to conjure up the glory and the doomed folly laid out in front of us.

> *At the Grand Finale, the Emperor led in person a charge of 30 or 40 squadrons of cavalry upon a long line of field guns in the centre of the enemy's position. We all galloped along in the greatest glee, and the surging waves of horsemen soon overwhelmed and swept through the rows of venomous-looking little cannons which presumed to confront them. 'Do you think it is all right?' we asked an Artillery Officer whose battery the Umpire had loyally adjudged to be captured. 'Certainly it is all right,' he replied. 'They are His Majesty's own guns. Why shouldn't he capture them? It is an honour for us to serve His Majesty in this manner.'*

Deauville 'dissipation' maybe, but here was the most serious of observers, and one who could conjure Shakespearian images with his pen.

'Upon how many of those who marched and cantered in that autumn sunlight,' he wrote after watching a second set of German manoeuvres three years later,

> *had the dark angel set his seal? Violent untimely death, ruin and humiliation worse than death, privations, mutiliations, despair to the simple soldier, the downfall of their pride and subsistence to the chiefs: such were the fates – could we have read them, which brooded over thousands and ten thousands of these virile figures.*
>
> *All the Kings and Princes of Germany, all the Generals of her Empire, clustered round the banqueting tables. Ten years were to see them scattered, exiled, deposed, in penury, in obloquy – the victims of a fatal system in which they were inextricably involved.*

It was a very Churchillian diagnosis, at least in hindsight, of a world preparing to go to disastrous war.

Churchill had maintained his military ties since early in the century, by joining his cousin and brother and many other friends, including F.E. Smith, as an officer in the Imperial Yeomanry, the forerunner of today's Territorial Army. On 2 January 1902, he was gazetted as a captain in the Queen's Own Oxfordshire Hussars, the local yeomanry regiment to Blenheim, with squadrons in Woodstock, Banbury, Henley and Oxford. Despite his Woodstock connections it was to the 80-strong Henley squadron, with its closer proximity to London, that Churchill devoted his attentions, starting with a drill session on 4 January that year, and climaxing with a summer camp for all of the 360 men of the regiment at Fawley Park, Henley from 25 May to 11 June.

F.E. Smith (later Lord Birkenhead), one of WSC's greatest friends

He had returned to the military with characteristic enthusiasm and diligence, writing detailed memos, sharpening up the mounted drill, and revelling in supremacy in the inter-squadron shooting competition. From 1902 to 1911 he only missed one year, 1904, of these fortnight-long summer camps held in the grounds of the great houses, and most splendidly at Blenheim. Consuelo Vanderbilt, the American heiress who in 1895 had married Sunny, the Duke of Marlborough – his family got the money, hers the title – remembered those weeks under canvas as 'a gay time with dinners and dances and sports. I remember an exciting paper chase which I won on a bay mare, thundering over the stone bridge up to the house in a dead heat with the adjutant.' Winston had been a favourite since she had met him first as a red-headed young man only a couple of years her senior. 'He struck me as ardent and vital,' she wrote in her memoirs, 'and seemed to have every intention of getting the most out of life, whether in sport, in love or in politics.'

In 1908, Winston, his squadron and their horses were in attendance at Wytham Abbey, the family seat of the Earl of Abingdon, just seven miles from Blenheim, but it's a wonder he had the time. First

The Churchill clan with the Oxfordshire Yeomanry. Sitting: 'Sunny', the Duke of Marlborough and Jack Churchill. Standing: Viscount Churchill and WSC

he had to clear his house of its tenant, the notorious racing figure Robert Sievier, who in 1902 had subjected the superb filly Sceptre to 12 top races in her three-year-old season, including twice at the short meeting at Newmarket, Epsom, Goodwood and Doncaster nevertheless winning four of the five classics, with only the Derby eluding her thanks to the incompetence of the jockey and the insanity of her owner/trainer. In April, Churchill accepted the full-on Cabinet post of President of the Board of Trade, and then failed to get re-elected for his Manchester seat, so had to stomp the streets of Dundee to ensure a new place in the Commons as a Liberal. In August he attended his brother Jack's wedding to Wytham Abbey's own Lady Gwendoline 'Goonie' Bertie.

But all this paled in comparison to what had happened to Winston in March, when he had arrived late for a dinner party in London and found his empty place next to the beautiful Clementine Hozier, who had struck him speechless on their first and only previous encounter four years earlier. This time Churchill freed his tongue and, despite previous failures with Pamela, Ethel and Muriel, and despite that Clementine had to decamp for two months to Germany, he managed to press his suit well enough to propose at Blenheim two days after Jack's wedding. Just a month later, on 12 September 1908, at St Margaret's, Westminster, he led the 23-year-old Miss Hozier down the aisle.

His life changed hugely for the better. Clementine had taken on, and was to deliver, a task few women in history would equal and none exceed. Anyone doubting the central importance of her role, or still picturing Churchill as a privileged, albeit multi-talented, political egotist should read the outpourings of love and concern and wisdom and argument in the stupendous volume of over 1,700 letters, notes and telegrams between Winston and Clemmie curated by their daughter Mary Soames. Clementine brought Winston many things, but high amongst them was a female companion to regale and to test, and sometimes a shoulder to cry on.

Clementine, 'My sweet and beloved Clemmie'

That need had always been clear in the long missives he sent to his mother. While those continued, the new correspondence came even closer to the heart. On 30 May 1909, six weeks before the birth of their first child, Diana, Winston is writing to his wife from Yeomanry camp in a letter which starts 'My Darling Sweet', contains many touching thoughts, and ends, 'Goodbye, my beloved Clemmie, I would so like to kiss your dear lips & to curl up snugly in your arms.' The confidences are not only loving ones. 'There were lots of soldiers & pseudo soldiers galloping about,' he adds jovially, before telling of the strange powers he feels within him. 'Do you know that I would greatly like to have some practice in the handling of large forces,' he tells her. 'I have much confidence in my judgement on things, when I see clearly, but on nothing do I seem to FEEL the truth more than in tactical combinations. It is a vain and foolish thing to say – but YOU will not laugh at it.'

Clementine would get used to wondering, worrying, suggesting, sharing, and above all revelling, in a partner whose love of life, and of her, jumps so warmly off the page. 'My sweet and beloved Clemmie', he wrote from the 1911 summer camp at Blenheim on 2 June, five days after their son Randolph had been born.

> The weather is gorgeous and the whole park is in gala glory.
> I have been out drilling all morning and my poor face is already
> a sufferer from the sun – the air however is deliciously cool.
> We have three regiments here, two just outside the ornamental
> gardens, & the third over by Bladon. Many congratulations
> are offered me upon the son. With that lack of jealousy which
> ennobles my nature, I lay them at your feet.

> I have 104 men in the squadron, & a very nice young officer –
> Valentine Fleming's youngest brother – 'the lesser flamingo'. FE is
> here and everything promises to be very pleasant. We are all going
> to bathe in the lake this evening. The water is said to be quite warm.

By now Clemmie would know how much Winston had enjoyed manoeuvres, and he would surely have told her his Kaiser stories from Silesia in 1906. She would have chuckled, as can we, as he describes how the QOOH (Queen's Own Oxfordshire Hussars – once unkindly dubbed as 'Queer Objects On Horseback') completed their Blenheim duties.

> We all marched past this morning – walk, trot & gallop. Jack &
> I took our squadrons at real pace and excited spontaneous plau-
> dits of the crowd. The Berkshires who followed could not keep
> up & grumbled. After the march past I made the General form
> the whole Brigade into Brigade Mass and gallop, 1,200-strong,
> the whole length of the park in one solid square of men and
> horses. It went awfully well.

Looking today at the photos of all these bewhiskered scions of stately houses gathered together for military jollies is likely to prompt only ridicule. What was it about moustaches? Jack Churchill's was nearly as big as that huge thing that made the bulgy-eyed Lord Randolph look like a King Charles spaniel. Sunny Marlborough had a curly-ended achievement that must have needed waxing twice a day. No doubt Winston would have grown one if he could, but the best he ever managed was a gingery stubble.

Those Oxfordshire gentry were of their time, of an age that would go patriotically to the slaughter in Flanders and, unlike many of today's über-rich, most of them accepted the deal that with power comes responsibility, and served their terms as magistrates, MPs and district chairmen. By their own standards they did their duty. Amongst several who would perish in the coming war would be Valentine Fleming of Brazier Park near Henley, which he would represent in Parliament from 1910 until being killed in Picardy in May 1917. When Valentine went to war in 1914 it was under the command of Sir Henry de Beauvoir de Lisle, formerly the mastermind of the Durham Light Infantry's dominance of Indian Polo. When Valentine died his obituary was written by Winston Churchill. When he is mentioned today it is as the father of Ian Fleming, the creator of James Bond.

Churchill, meanwhile, was taking on heavier and heavier political duties. In February 1910 he was made Home Secretary. In October 1911, he became First Lord of the Admiralty. The constant flow of letters between Winston and Clemmie dealt with the highest issues of state and the smallest intimacies of family life. On 26 October 1909, Winston writes to Clementine, then staying with a nanny and baby Diana at a hotel in Crowborough to escape London for what was then termed 'Scotland in Sussex', to report a typically frenetic 'Churchill in Westminster' routine – he had been finishing a book (*Liberalism and the Social Problem*), there had been discussions on Somaliland, and he had been arraigned by a titled supporter of the Suffragettes only slightly less intemperate than the woman who a month later would attack him with a dog whip on Bristol Station and, but for Clementine grabbing him, would have pushed him off the platform.

But then he revealed an intriguing new element in their partnership.

'It is such fun riding with you,' the letter continues, 'and when you are able to gallop really fast over beautiful turf it will be a great joy to us both.'

The next day he reiterates his pleasure. 'I did enjoy my Sunday with you. And you rode so well this morning. As soon as you come back to London you must order a habit and then riding lessons in earnest. Almost immediately you could ride in the Row with me on a quiet meek horse.'

A week later Clementine is replying, 'I have found a lovely new ride for us on Saturday.' It was a touching enthusiasm from a woman

who was as athletic as she was intelligent. Despite bouts of ill
health and mental exhaustion, she was an enthusiastic golfer and
fine tennis player, but clearly got great reward from her early days
on horseback.

It was probably in Clemmie's genes, because many people,
most importantly her daughter Mary Soames, have suggested that
her real father was not the elderly and absent Sir Henry Hozier,
but the dashing cavalier 'Bay' Middleton, with whom the flirty Lady
Blanche had been conducting an affair at the time of conception. Bay,
who first came into our story when squiring the galloping Empress of
Austria over the banks of County Meath, had been killed in 1892 when
his horse turned over on the flat when well clear in a steeplechase in
Warwickshire. He was buried – you might not be surprised to know –
in his full riding gear.

By the winter of 1911–12, Clementine was adept enough to have
taken to hunting with gusto, either up in Leicestershire with Freddy
Guest at Burley-on-the-Hill, or with the Heythrop from Blenheim,
from where on 3 January 1912 she wrote:

Clementine, a keen sportswoman

My Darling.

*I have just come back from a long day's hunting – The meet was
at Stow-on-the-Wold, 25 miles away. It was the greatest fun –
Sunny took charge of me & gave me a hand over the stone walls –
We found at once and had a lovely run over the vale. Sunny took
me out of the crowd on one side & all morning we were at the
top of the hunt. We went over some quite big places. I took all the
fences after Sunny. No one was in at the death but Captain Daly
gave me the brush.*

Contemporary custom in Britain recoils at such trophies –
Winston had been so rewarded after his first day's hunting from
Blenheim on Boxing Day, 1895. Yet such traditions lasted right
through until the 1960s: I remember the walls of our house festooned,
like so many of its type, with mounted fox's brushes (tails), and indeed
'masks', as their stuffed heads were called, with the inscription of
time and place, and often the actual minutes of the hunt.

Of all the pictures of Winston and Clementine, none beats that
of the pair of them riding together in October 1913 at some military
manoeuvres near Daventry. They are happy, young, confident, and
easy in the saddle. Clementine had cracked it, albeit, as was the custom with young ladies of her class, having to do so side-saddle.

In 1906 Pamela Plowden, writing to Winston about borrowing one
of his polo ponies for the winter, had told him excitedly how she was
learning to ride astride, but in April 1908 Jack Churchill was thanking
his wife Goonie for ceasing something he considered quite scandalous:
'You know girls who do that sort of thing, only do it to show their legs…

if I felt that you, Darling, whom I love so much, were doing such things in front of others, I should be so unhappy and most frightfully angry.'

This most bizarre and prudish of customs continued even after the First World War: in 1921 when my normally strong-minded mother, who had ridden astride all her youth in the Isle of Wight, came up to hunt with my father in Gloucestershire, she was firmly told that it would have to be side-saddle, and she meekly went off to have lessons with the groom.

At the beginning of August 1914, German troops crossed the Belgian border, and at midnight on the 4th, Britain issued its ultimatum to Germany to respect Belgian neutrality. Europe was now at war. Churchill's energy and combativeness soon made him a driving force in Asquith's wartime Cabinet, but by Christmas, as history knows, hostilities had locked down into the stalemate of trench warfare all along the Western Front.

In the face of this, Churchill was a natural champion for the original, but in the event doomed, initiative of opening an Eastern Front in early 1915 with the idea of taking the Dardanelles Strait, knocking out Turkey and opening up a supply line to Russia, and it is still arguable that he was made a scapegoat for the disasters that followed: battleships sunk by mines in the Strait, and invading troops slaughtered in their thousands on the beaches of Gallipoli. He left the Admiralty on 23 May, and his largely titular post as Chancellor of the Duchy of Lancaster, on 11 November. Anyone wishing to depict him as little more than a heartless warmonger (one of the lesser epithets at the time), however, should heed the tone of the handwritten letter he sent in reply to one of Jack Seely's, then commanding a dismounted Canadian Cavalry Brigade in the trenches near Ypres, with Churchill's young protégé Archibald Sinclair as his ADC:

> It is odious to me to remain here watching sloth and folly with full knowledge and no occupation.
>
> I was deeply touched by the very great kindness of your letter. I hope you will not go beyond the line of duty sportingly conceived in going into danger. Do not seek peril beyond what is necessary to discharge your full task, and do not get Archie into trouble.
>
> God bless you and guard you both is the hope and prayer of your faithful friend,
>
> W.

Within a week of leaving the Cabinet, Winston was in France. He had volunteered, and been accepted, for a commission on the front line, and by 20 November he was attached for training with a detachment of Grenadier Guards, who at the start were as deeply sceptical of him as the battalion of Royal Scots Fusiliers which he and his now ADC Archie Sinclair joined on 3 January. Their somewhat unconventional arrival allowed one of its officers to provide a rare and mannered glimpse of him on horseback at this time.

'Just before noon,' wrote F.D. Scott,

an imposing cavalcade arrived. Churchill on a black charger, Archie Sinclair on a black charger, two grooms on black chargers followed by a limber filled with Churchill's baggage – much more than the 35 pounds allowed weight. In the rear half we saw a curious contraption: a long bath and boiler for heating the hot water.

What followed was described as 'quite the most uncomfortable lunch I have ever been at', during which Churchill stared at each officer in turn and ended with this uncompromising peroration: 'Gentlemen, I am now your commanding officer. Those who support me I shall look after. Those who go against me I will break. Good afternoon, gentlemen.'

Uncompromising he may have been; unsuccessful he was not. Quite soon he was winning round both the officers, who were able to use his bath, and men who, just like Sergeant Hallaway in the 4th Hussars and Sergeant Reeve in the 17th Lancers, were impressed by his tireless and inventive efforts at improving their conditions as well as their efficiency. Faced with the absolute he did something which will win any man over. With his fearless forays into No Man's Land, he showed that he would die for them. Twenty-four years later the whole nation would feel the same.

Despite all this, it was in politics that his war would have to be fought, and it was a deeply disappointed regiment that wished him goodbye on 6 May 1916 for his return to Westminster where, after an uphill battle trying to protect his reputation in front of the Dardanelles Commission, he finally re-entered the government in 1917 under Lloyd George as Minister of Munitions.

Even now Churchill did not lose touch with horses altogether. Clementine saw to that. She had never hunted with any frequency after that 1911–12 season, but her enjoyment of riding, and her wish for Winston to continue in his love of it, remained. Even on 9 August 1914, five days after war has been declared, she was desperate to offer hope to an embattled Winston up to his ears as First Lord of the Admiralty. 'My Dear One', she writes from a holiday cottage in Cromer, 'I have such a good idea – Later on, in the spring when perhaps we could afford a motor again, let's instead have two chestnut horses "with nice long tails" & ride for an hour every morning. It would be of far more value to you than a motor & I should enjoy it so much.'

When Winston could only manage a frazzled five-line reply she realised that idyllic dreams were not enough: 'My own Darling, I feel such a note of fatigue in your letter. Now are you doing everything you can not to be too tired?' The danger of exhaustion for politicians remains as real as ever – how can it make sense that the most important and dangerous decisions in the world are often taken by politicians utterly sleep-deprived or jet-lagged?

Clementine's three-point solution was exceedingly practical. The third point was not smoking too much. The second was 'Going to bed before midnight... you MUST have 8 hours sleep a night to be your best self.' But her number one imperative was: 'Never missing your morning ride.'

Government ministers today are occasionally pictured jogging in St James's Park kitted out in unflattering track suits. For Winston Churchill it was snappy hacking gear and a canter round Hyde Park. I know which would be more photogenic. In May 1908 Rotten Row had been so crowded, and the mounted gentry so goggle-eyed at a lady with a slit up the thigh of her side-saddle riding habit, that one of them had trotted straight into Winston. He would still be riding out in the Row when the war was over.

WSC with General John French, the future Commander-in-Chief

14

BATTLING ON,
1918–1945

"Abruptly he sees his chance, and
he gathers his pony and charges in,
neither deft nor graceful but full of
tearing physical energy – and skilful
with it too. He bears down opposition
by the weight of his dash, and strikes
the ball. Did I say strike? He slashes
the ball."

Today's soldiers are beginning to face the psychological effects of the trauma of war. Back then, men and ministers had to handle it as best they could. In the case of Churchill after the end of the First World War, this naturally involved getting back in the swing of riding, buying polo ponies and becoming a playing member at Roehampton. His love of the saddle and the chase comes through vividly in letters he sent to Clementine on consecutive days at the end of March. To ease an over-active mind he had also become an enthusiastic painter: 'an added interest to every common scene, an occupation for every idle hour, an unceasing voyage of entrancing discovery'.

His political duties continued to get more arduous as he was made Secretary of State for War and was immediately confronted with Russia in revolution and the problems of demobilisation. How much support to give the anti-Bolshevik forces, and how to handle more than a million troops coming back from France, were of course the greatest problems, but horses were not forgotten.

When Churchill discovered that only 3,000, instead of the promised 12,000, a week of the horses who had been used in the war effort on the Western Front – to pull supply carts, to haul transports conveying soldiers' bodies, or indeed for officers like Churchill to ride in the front line – were being shipped back across the Channel, Lieutenant General Sir Travers Clarke, the Quartermaster-General, got a letter he would not forget:

> *If it is so serious, what are you doing about it? The letter of the Commander in Chief discloses a complete failure on the part of the Ministry of Shipping to meet its obligations, and scores of thousands of horses will be left in France under extremely disadvantageous conditions.*

The numbers quickly trebled, but the terrible statistics remain, that of the million horses sent out from Britain during the war only 100,000 returned. One of the luckiest ones was my grandfather's thoroughbred Warrior, who first landed in France in August 1914 and survived Ypres, the Somme, Passchendaele and Cambrai, to lead a thousand-strong charge of the Canadian Cavalry on 30 March 1918, return home to win a race at the Isle of Wight Point in 1922, and live right through to 1941. On 2 September 2014 he was awarded 'the animals' VC', the PDSA Dickin Medal, to honour all the animals who served in the Great War.

But for Churchill it was a case of busy men get busier. From 1920 he was acting as Colonial Secretary with responsibility for the Middle East, while also retaining a role as mediator in the long-running feud in Ireland between nationalists and unionists – and not forgetting the four children he had by now, or the multi-volume history he planned to write of the recent conflict.

WSC rides Western Style at Calgary 1929

Yes he was never the modern idea of a workaholic. For instance, when the anti-Bolshevik forces were collapsing in March 1920, Churchill was off to south-west France with General Henry Rawlinson, remembered from an exhausted day during the collapse of the Fifth Army in 1918. They were to visit the Duke of Westminster's villa at Mimizan, south of Bordeaux, for a few days' riding, painting and, as it was with the Duke, hunting the wild boar.

'We did not succeed in securing a pen wiper' (Churchill's nickname for wild boar), he wrote on 26 March, 'though we were within two minutes of one and the hounds yelped like mad. We were riding pretty hard for five hours and I am not at all tired. We got back here in time to paint a nice picture.' The following day sounds a touch more peaceful.

The General [Rawlinson] *and I are entirely alone here, and we lead a very simple life divided entirely between riding, painting and eating. As the hounds will not be fit for hunting till Monday we went for a long ride this morning down to the sea; over two hours at a pretty good pace. I had a splendid horse – a different one to the one I hunted yesterday; an enormous black English hunter with a head and shoulder which made you feel as if you were on the bridge of a battle cruiser... Three quarters of an hour's ride brought us to the sea. Most lovely sands are spread out for miles. There was, as is usual here, a fine display of breakers, seven or eight great walls of foam advancing one on top of the other. We rode our horses into the surf up to their hocks, and so for a couple of miles along the beach and back for lunch.*

Riding horses along the beach is a blissful pleasure and, if you do it at full gallop, is one of splendid, windswept, salty excitement – one of my best mounted memories is riding the legendary Red Rum along the sands at Southport before the third of his record victories in the Grand National – the drumming of the hooves beneath you, the creaming of the waves on the shore.

But Churchill's post-war life retained something of the soaring and crashing trajectory that had characterised his war years, leaving his 'highly strung' personality at risk of sinking into a 'Black Dog' depression. Family life had been besieged by financial worries, but 1921 began with a touch of magnificent good fortune for the ever-extravagant spender, when a distant relative, Lord Henry Vane-Tempest Stewart, died in a railway accident. As he was unmarried, the Garron Tower estate in County Antrim, Northern Ireland, plus paintings and emeralds passed to Winston. The inheritance came through his great-grandmother Frances Vane-Tempest Stewart, who had been married to the 7th Duke of Marlborough, and was also the sister of the Countess of Portarlington at Emo Court in Ireland, where Winston had fallen off his donkey back in 1879. Churchill found himself the beneficiary of an income worth £4,000 a year, or a cool £160,000 in today's money.

Clementine was wary, no doubt with good reason, of what her husband might do with the money. 'Darling,' she wrote, 'let us beware of risking our newly come fortune in operations we do not understand & have not the time to learn & to practise when learnt. Politics are absolutely engrossing to you really, or SHOULD be, & now you have Painting for your leisure & Polo for your excitement and danger.'

Polo for a thickening man in his late forties was not without its dangers, but Clementine clearly saw it as infinitely better than her husband's passion for flying, which had involved several narrow escapes before, during and after the war, most recently an awful crash at Croydon which had ended with two broken legs for the pilot, and would have been the end of both flyers if he hadn't managed to switch off the fuel supply seconds before he got knocked unconscious.

Soon that same year, however, came very real tragedy. April 1921 saw the suicide of Clementine's brother Bill, aged 34. In June was the passing of Winston's mother Jennie, at the age of 67. Winston also lost his faithful valet Thomas Walden. Worst of all, in August, was the ever-jagged wound of the loss of their adored daughter Marigold, 'Duckadilly', from septicaemia, at just two and a half.

Through all this, and through all his much more public tribula-tions, there was a constant shelter which Churchill both guarded and sought: the love of family and friends – and many of those friendships had been made on horseback.

Roger Keyes is a perfect example. He and Winston had first met playing polo at Roehampton in 1904. As Chief of Staff to the naval commander of the Dardanelles campaign he had been the closest of allies. After Churchill bought Chartwell in August 1922, the hill-top manor house in Kent, Keyes would join his friend riding in the Kent countryside.

Churchill craved comradeship. You see it in his subaltern days in India, with Barnes and Baring and the rest. It is obvious in his evident enjoyment of the long saddle-borne hours on the veldt described in *Ian Hamilton's March*, and it is clear in the way he holds on to cross-party friendships despite hurling the strongest of insults across the chamber. In 1911 he and F.E. Smith, the closest of friends and strongest of opponents, had formed the Other Club, with the express purpose of bringing MPs from different parties to dine together once a fortnight, but with the rather over-elaborate rider: 'Nothing in the rules or intercourse of the Club shall interfere with the rancour or asperity of party politics.'

The tribulations of 1921 also made Winston keen to get back into polo. But in April 1922, while staying at Eaton Hall in Cheshire

House of Commons team for the polo match versus the House of Lords. WSC stands next to his cousin Freddy Guest, and fellow MPs Captain G.R.G. Shaw and Captain Euan Wallace with the ever-generous Duke of Westminster, he had the most unusual of crashes. 'My dear Fred,' he wrote to his cousin and political colleague Freddy Guest,

> *I shall not be right for some weeks, never having had a worse fall from a pony. I was dismounting on the offside – a slovenly touch which I have used thousands of times with impunity – and at the critical moment the pony gave a most violent bound & I fell plumb on my shoulder, knocking all the wind and nearly knocking the life out of me.*

Badly shaken he may have been, but he still joined Freddy in that year's Commons team, which lost to a Lords' 'équipe' that included the Duke of Westminster, Freddy's brother Ivor, who as Lord Wimborne had been Lord Lieutenant of Ireland at the time of the 1916 Easter Rising, and the Prince of Wales. The Commons lost 3-4, but the strain of recent events, coupled with the political pressure that at times led him to sleep with his revolver beside him for fear of IRA assassination, was beginning to tell on Winston.

'The doctors think that it is too much for me to play polo this year in addition to all my work and after my fall,' he wrote to Colonel Edward Miller at Roehampton on 5 July.

> *I find myself so exhausted after a match, and it takes me three days to get back to normal. It is a great disappointment to me, but I must submit. Will you therefore kindly send the grey pony McEwen and the bay pony Hindoo to Sir Archibald Sinclair, who will keep them and play them for the rest of the season. Will you also send the bay Jorrocks and the other little grey, whose name I forget, to Mrs Chapman's stable at No. 6 Somers Mews, Gloucester Square, Hyde Park, W2, so that I can ride them in the mornings in the Row. Thank you for all the help you have given me. I do not despair of playing next year.*

Admiral of the Fleet, Roger Keyes, who hosted WSC's last polo game in Malta, January 1927

Despair never did have a place in the Winston Churchill song-book. Despite the collapse of the Liberal Party and the loss of his own Dundee seat in the November General Election soon after his most recent hospitalisation, leaving him memorably 'without an office, without a seat, without a party and without an appendix,' he upped sticks with the family to Villa Rève d'Or near Cannes to work on his five-volume memoir of the First World War, *The World Crisis*, and when the first volume was ready he sent a copy to the Prince of Wales with a note that he was getting active again.

'I am so glad to hear that you have had a lot of polo and are fit enough again to enjoy it,' replied the Prince on 12 April 1923.

WSC and the then Edward Prince of Wales at polo

It's great news to hear you are playing in London this coming season & I hope we get lots of games together. I shan't have time to play seriously so shall only compete in 'station games' such as we had two years ago. I've had a lot of fun race riding and it is sad that it and the hunting are all over.

Winston did get going that year, and at the beginning of the next, his 50th. Amongst those at Roehampton, reported the *Bystander*, were 'Mr Winston Churchill, who seems hardly less keen on the game than he was in his subaltern days in India'. In 'a big game' at Roehampton in June it noted that Winston 'turned out displaying undiminished energy'. 'He rides in the game like heavy cavalry getting into position for the assault,' wrote Patrick Thompson at the time.

He trots about, keenly watchful, biding his time, a matter of tactics and strategy. Abruptly he sees his chance, and he gathers his pony and charges in, neither deft nor graceful but full of tearing physical energy – and skilful with it too. He bears down opposition by the weight of his dash, and strikes the ball. Did I say strike? He slashes the ball.

All this was crowned, after two bruising by-election defeats, first as a candidate for the fading Liberals, then as an independent, with a triumph for Winston at the General Election in Epping, standing as a 'Constitutionalist' with full Conservative support, believing that only the Tories were strong enough to stand up to the threat of Communism. Congratulations came from some felicitous sources: Pamela Plowden in Darjeeling, where her husband Victor, Lord Lytton had been putting down a little local difficulty as the Governor of Bengal; T.E. Lawrence – 'This isn't congratulations, it's just the hiss of my excess delight rushing out'; and, the ultimate example of old bonds being firmest, from Reggie Barnes, now living down in the West Country. 'My dear old Winston,' wrote his companion from India and way back in Cuba,

> *I am SO glad & so is everyone else – barring the Bolshies. Well done old Friend, it is a comfort to think that anyhow there is some-one in the House who has the guts to stick up for the old Flag. Make me one of your private secretaries when you are PM will you!*
>
> *Best love, & I hope to see you again soon. Don't bother to answer this if you are too busy.*
>
> *Your old pal*
> *Reggie*

In November of that year Churchill's career hit a new high, when Prime Minister Stanley Baldwin asked him to be Chancellor of the Exchequer in the Conservative government, just as Lord Randolph had been 38 years earlier, and the following April, 1925, Winston presented his first Budget, a task his father had failed to stay long enough to achieve. Nothing, however, prevented him from turning out once more in the Lords v Commons match.

However, in August of that year, Churchill wrote to Jack Wodehouse, now the Earl of Kimberley, to tell him he was giving up polo, and asking him to help sell his ponies. 'It is dreadful giving it up for ever,' wrote Winston, his fears for his workload were well founded, for the following year, 1926, was to prove one of the hardest and bitterest of Churchill's whole career. To the long running miners' strike was added in May the short-lived but nationally divisive General Strike to which Winston started as the most bellicose of opponents although later being at the centre of the government's efforts at settlement. For, despite many public, much resented prods at the mine owners, he still failed to get them to back down from their determination to cut wages, and the exhausted miners returned to work with the feeling that Winston had betrayed them.

The ramifications of those failed negotiations must have been very painful. Churchill had distinguished himself as a progressive Home Secretary and a humane Chancellor, but when all his efforts, and there had been many, to make the mine owners settle had ended in failure, a delegation from the miners' union came to see him. 'We understood you were a man of courage,' said Herbert Smith, their president, 'but you have broken down at the first fence. You have dismounted.' However unfair the criticism, the riding metaphor would have cut to the quick.

But life, and books, and indeed holidays had to go on. Winston had just finished the third, highly lauded volume of his war memoirs, and over the previous four years had been the driving force in the landscaping of the grounds at Chartwell in almost Capability Brown fashion. Now it was time for a break.

The holiday would take in Genoa and Vesuvius, and see his 15-year-old son Randolph come with him, along with his own brother Jack. They would return via Rome, where Winston would meet and be charmed by Mussolini, before spending four days on the Riviera, then entraining north for a big political lunch in Paris, and closing off with three days' boar hunting at the Chateau de St-Saens near Dieppe with his friend the Duke of Westminster, and 'Bend'Or''s latest mistress, Coco Chanel.

Roger Keyes was now the Admiral commanding the Mediterranean fleet based in Malta, and when he heard that Winston was planning a trip to Italy and France he insisted his old friend come over to the island. And while he was there – how about a game of polo? The subsequent correspondence is a charming example of how, even with all the weighty responsibilities both men then carried, camaraderie still shone through.

WSC with Randolph, Coco Chanel and the Duke of Westminster's boar hounds at St-Saens in January 1927

'As to polo', Churchill wrote on 15 November 1926, some 18 months after that supposed final Lords v Commons performance,

of course I would love to have a game. It is awfully kind of you to offer to mount me. It would have to be a mild one, as I have not played all this season. However, I will arrange to have a gallop or two beforehand so as to 'calibrate' my tailor muscles. Anyhow, I will bring a couple of sticks and do my best. If I expire on the ground it will at any rate be a worthy end!

Keyes is soon into arrangements: no need to bring sticks, four chukkas would probably be enough, and what's Winston's Hurlingham handicap (higher is better, the reverse of golf)? The reply comes back, typically mixing business with pleasure, suggesting that they play on Saturday 8th, the day after he arrives: 'I thought it might be inconvenient to play on the Monday, as you state the Fleet would probably be sailing that day. You must realise that I am very bad at Polo. I think my latest handicap is two.'

On Christmas Eve 1926 Churchill was still at a wintry Chartwell, but looking forward to the Maltese sunshine. 'I shall be with you in plenty of time to play on Saturday afternoon (Jan 8),' he wrote. 'I do not think one day's practice will do me much good. I hope to do a little hacking in the next few days, if the snow which now overlays us should permit.'

Malta was no bad place for a last hurrah. The polo ground there would have seen battle with many invaders before England took over from Napoleon's forces in 1800, and the island was to have an even tougher time in the Second World War. But on 8 January 1927 it was a polo contest that mattered. Winston Churchill was 52 years old, and for the last three had been Chancellor of the Exchequer, in a political career which had risen to new heights after crashing into seeming ruin and revulsion over his role in the disaster of the Dardanelles in 1915.

There is no official report of how the four chukkas went on the island, but on 14 January Roger Keyes wrote to a friend to tell him that 'Winston played extraordinarily well considering he has not played for two years.' Winston sent a proud little note to Clementine. 'I got through polo without shame or distinction & did enjoy it so much.' It was the last match he would ever play.

After the polo had finished there was not a lot of riding in Churchill's life, bar trips down to the Duke of Westminster's Chateau de St-Saens for boar hunting; on occasions both Randolph and Clementine came. In March 1931 Charlie Chaplin accepted Bend'Or's invitation to St-Saens, but had a mixed day in the saddle and said he could not sit down for a week afterwards – no doubt a story told with considerable glee and gusto when Charlie was a guest at Chartwell six months later.

Another guest boar hunting with the Duke of Westminster, Charlie Chaplin. Afterwards he said he could not sit down for a week!

Charlie Chaplin at Chartwell with WSC
in 1931

That St-Saens was one of Churchill's favourite retreats, and
that at 62 Winston was acquiring a tiny bit of physical prudence,
is confirmed in the letter he sent in December 1936 to the Duke of
Windsor just a week after the new king's abdication as Edward VIII:

*Bend'Or would be delighted if you could use St-Saens. His
horses and hounds are there and every facility for the chase.
I do not know whether your R.H. has ever hunted the boar. It is
pretty good sport, and I like it because although there is a great
deal of rough and tricky riding through woodland and up and
down hill, there are no fences to jump.*

But if not horses, there was a lot of everything else. Churchill
presented two more Budgets as Chancellor of the Exchequer, and
then found himself out of office for what we are invited to call his

'lost decade'. He was hardly out of action. During it he wrote half
a dozen more books. Projects just spouted from that hyperactive
brain. 'Building a cottage and dictating a book,' he wrote to Prime
Minister Stanley Baldwin in September 1928, '200 bricks and 2,000
words a day.' A cottage was one of countless plans and endless
expenditure around Chartwell that included all sorts of landscaping,
and a menagerie of animals from farm cattle to pigs to black swans
to butterflies. He toured America, lost a big whack on Wall Street,
and was knocked down by a car on fifth Avenue. As David Lough so
splendidly chronicles in his riveting history of Churchill's finances,
No More Champagne, there was little stinting in the cellar, and the
Churchill finances were in a perpetual state of flux as he tried to write
more books or risk new stock market adventures to bail himself out
of trouble. The books went from the amazing six-volume history of
the First World War through the wry and thrilling *My Early Life* to the
magisterial four-volume biography of his ancestor the first Duke of
Marlborough. When the brain wanted a rest it was switched to long
hours outside with paint brush and easel.

   And then, in September 1939, Hitler invaded Poland, and the
world was at war again, and in May 1940 Churchill became Prime
Minister, vowing to lead Britain and the free world in standing firm
against the Nazis, and able to offer 'nothing… but blood, toil, tears and
sweat'. It would be the most extraordinary and remarkable period, not
only in Churchill's life, but also in British history. And there we have
to leave Winston for fully five years, until the war would finally be
won, with, of course, no time for riding horses.

   Except there is one tiny glimpse that the memory of their magic
had not left him.

   Douglas Russell, in his uniquely informative book *Winston
Churchill, Soldier*, relates a wartime story from Mary Soames,
Winston's youngest daughter. It was 1943, and the great man was
returning by sea from Canada, having met President Roosevelt
in Quebec in the build-up to the Teheran conference with Stalin
in November to agree the opening of a second front against Nazi
Germany. On the voyage back across the Atlantic on HMS *Renown*,
baffled onlookers found themselves watching and listening to the war
leader of the Western world, and one of the greatest political figures
in modern history, manoeuvring himself about the quarter-deck to
explain the intricacies of cavalry drill.

WSC giving advice to the future Duke
of Windsor

15

HORSES AGAIN, 1946–51

"I'm still the man I was."

The iconic White Cliffs of Dover were just 50 miles away. The horse was called Geronimo. The place was Chartwell Farm in Kent. The date was 27 November 1948, three and a half years since the nation-wide celebrations at the end of the Second World War. The man who had led Britain to V-for-Victory in 1945 had then been ejected by the voters in the Labour landslide of the subsequent election but, far from leaving the fray, was now Leader of the Opposition. In three days' time the big chief would be 74, and he needed to show there was life in the old dog yet. More to the point, he had not been out with the hunt for more than a decade. By now even hunting had its political side: the first Anti-Field Sports Bill was in the offing. So it was a rum punch, a big cigar, and 'Tally-ho!'

It was a visitor to Chartwell in October 1946 who had tempted him back into the saddle. Jan Van Leer was a circus owner specialising in white Lipizzaner horses, whose dancing skills apparently included both the waltz and the polka. Van Leer was also a Churchill fan and, according to the report in *Life* magazine, asked and was granted permission to come to Chartwell and show a couple of his horses. 'Unable to resist one called Salve,' *Life* related, 'Churchill, who had not ridden for ten years, went off for a ten-minute canter and found that it did his liver good. "I'm still the man I was," he said.' The photos confirm it.

That he returned to the saddle after this caper seems to be confirmed by the report of Churchill's hunting day in 1948 in *Sphere* magazine. Geronimo is described as the horse 'which he frequently used for hacking', while in the photograph Churchill's riding gear looks well used, but hardly cut for the leaner polo-playing physique of yesteryear. More importantly, the Lipizzaners had also been ridden by his daughter Mary, who had been so keen on riding as a girl that she had been given a chestnut mare called Patsy as a reward for brilliant results in her School Certificate, and much of her teenage leisure time was spent at the famed Sam Marsh's nearby Scamperdale Livery Stables, from where Geronimo hailed.

In many ways this final saddle-borne memory of Winston Churchill is as remarkable as any in the long chain of four-legged associates, from that Irish donkey to the last polo pony under the Maltese sun. It stretched the bounds of credibility that the sickly child, the weedy youth, the impetuous soldier, the embattled politician and the infinitely stressed war leader should be galloping off with the Old Surrey and Burstow with no ailments worse than the shoulder damaged in 1896, and an over-indulged frame that was now a good 13 stone on the bathroom scales.

Yet here he was in the snappiest matching jacket, waistcoat and jodhpurs, riding along with the best of them. What's more, horses were about to become part of his world in a major new way. Within six months he would buy his first racehorse and his final years would be spent deriving huge pleasure, and very considerable success, by following his father's example on the turf.

In February 1947 Mary had married the former soldier, future
Cabinet minister and one-time winner of a wartime version of the
Italian Grand National, Christopher Soames, and came to live at the
adjoining Chartwell Farm. A year later it was Christopher who got
Sam Marsh to buy him a 20-year-old mare called Pannikin that then
produced a foal to be named Loving Cup, who would eventually win
a race for his father-in-law in 1952.

Entranced by having mares and foals around the place, and with
his finances safer now that Chartwell had been purchased for the
nation, Churchill wanted horses of his own. Soames found another
mare called Poetic, who was to become the dam of a good winner
called Prince Arthur, and a filly foal by Vigorous, out of Gallant Girl,
that was to be wittily named as Moll Flanders.

As well as pre-figuring the future, all this harked back strangely
to the past. For in 1947 Churchill had written a short story called 'The
Dream'. The dream in question was an encounter with the ghost of
Lord Randolph, which had appeared whilst Winston was painting
his portrait in the studio at Chartwell. In the story Lord Randolph
gets Churchill to tell him what has happened since his death in 1895
and the narrative closes with a cryptic smile: 'As I listened to you
unfolding these fearful facts you seemed to know a great deal about
them,' says the father to his always underrated son. 'I never expected

WSC and his daughter Mary ride
Jan Van Leer's circus horses at Chartwell
in October 1946

you would develop so far and so fully. Of course you are too old now to think about such things, but when I hear you talk I really wonder why you didn't go into politics. You might have done a lot to help. You might even have made a name for yourself.'

But long before that pay-off line, one of the first things the father asks in the story is, 'Does the Turf Club exist? And racing?'

'It all goes on,' replies Winston.

'What, the Oaks, the Derby and the Leger?'

'They have never missed a year.'

Winston's parenting may have been unorthodox, not to say dysfunctional, by today's standards, but there is no doubt that Jennie and Randolph left the deepest of impressions, and who is to say that he wasn't reaching towards them in his diversions? He had long found precious solace in the painting at which his mother had so excelled, and now, in old age, he was about to re-register the chocolate-and-pink racing silks in which L'Abbesse De Jouarre had won the Oaks all those years ago.

Lord Randolph's actual colours, and those worn by Winston in those pony scurries in India, were chocolate, pink sleeves and cap, but as these were now too similar to someone else's, Churchill had to settle for pink, chocolate sleeves and cap when they were finally registered in June 1949.

No such hitches in the purchase and handling of Colonist II, the first and most famous of runners that Winston was to have over the next 15 years. Buying horses for a father-in-law's amusement sounds a good idea, but it all too often ends in wrangling, untold expense and disillusionment. In recent times, Lord Oaksey's daughter and son-in-law Sarah and Mark Bradstock did wonders in getting that great but ageing racing figure a mare called Plaid Maid, who won five steeple-chases and then bred three good winners, including the Gold Cup hero Coneygree. But they still don't hold a candle to what Christopher Soames and his ally, the astute and well-connected Epsom vet Arnold Carey Foster, pulled off for Winston Churchill.

The plot must have been hatching for some time. Certainly since Carey Foster saw a big, plain-looking but good-moving, wall-eyed grey called Colonist II run second in a small race at Le Tremblay near Paris in April 1949, and bought him on behalf of Walter Nightingall who trained at the impressive South Hatch stables his grandfather John Nightingall had built in 1860 half a mile down the hill from Epsom racecourse. Walter had recently saddled the 1,000th winner since taking over from his father in 1926, and had long enjoyed a rep-utation as much for integrity and kindness as for undoubted achieve-ment. No bad ally for Soames, and his role was certainly fully planned in the quite masterly letter he wrote to his father-in-law on 23 July 1949: 'You will remember when Walter Nightingall came over here the other day,' the letter starts, 'he told you he had a horse just over from France which he thought might prove a good one. He was going to try

WSC on Salve, October 1946. 'I'm still the man I was.'

it out with some good horses and, if he thought it good enough, he was going to let you have first refusal.' From that opening we know that Christopher had already got Walter across from Epsom to meet his father-in-law and Walter had, as all well-briefed trainers would most certainly have – 'just the horse for you'.

The letter confirms how much Christopher was in on the act. 'He galloped it today,' the son-in-law continues about the potential purchase,

> *and asked me over to watch it. It was accompanied by three good horses, all of which have won middle-class races. It put up a most impressive display. Although it finished second, it was going much the best at the finish, and beat by eight lengths a horse which has won its last three races.*
>
> *I consider that this horse will turn into a really good one which might well win valuable races next year, and I would be most surprised if it did not win two or three small races this year. The price is £1,600, and it will in my view be worth £2,000 after it has won one race. If you are contemplating buying a horse in training I think it would be very difficult to find such a good-looking horse with such possibilities at so cheap a price.*

Christopher Soames was on the verge of a very distinguished career in public service, including eight years in Cabinet office, shadow Foreign Secretary and, not least, a fine stint as British Ambassador in Paris (which once included the minor but much appreciated duty of visiting me in the ambulance room after I had been knocked out in a hurdle race at Auteuil racecourse). But nothing bettered what Soames did with Colonist, who proceeded to deliver at the very first time of asking. This was on 23 August, at Salisbury, and the colt must have impressed the touts at Epsom beforehand as he started hot favourite, with 'Young Randolph' (now aged 38) in the grandstand.

The father had been characteristically overdoing things. In a year spent badgering away at the Labour Party as Leader of the Opposition, he had also travelled to Brussels to speak on establishing a European Court of Human Rights, and to America to pledge support for the newly formed NATO (North Atlantic Treaty Organization). He was now down in the south of France dictating the fourth volume of his war memoirs and, most unwisely, showing off to actress Merle Oberon by doing somersaults in the surf and receiving a minor stroke for his pains. 'The news has cheered me up no end,' he replied to Randolph's cable telling of Colonist's victory. 'I feel a lot better already.'

Well enough to see Colonist win next time at Windsor on 11 September, St Leger day , and then on 22 September to be on hand to watch the colt go for the hat-trick in the Ribblesdale Stakes (a race not then confined, as now, to fillies) at Ascot in front of the renowned racing writer Geoffrey Gilbey. Back in December 1926 Gilbey, along with Churchill's South African colleague J.B. Atkins, now editor of the *Spectator*, had been part of a deputation to the then Chancellor of the Exchequer in favour of Betting Tax, and had concluded that Churchill had little interest or knowledge of the game. Not now: 'Colonist II drew further and further away to win with his ears pricked,' wrote Gilbey. 'I ran with many others to the unsaddling enclosure to greet the return of the colt who had scored the most popular victory I have ever seen on a racecourse.'

To many this seemed an unrepeatable moment, especially as in his next race Colonist got beaten, after hanging badly right on the left-handed circuit at Lingfield, to spawn chuckling headlines ranging from the *Sporting Life*'s COLONIST IS NOT LEFT WINGER to the *New York Sun*'s CHURCHILL'S HORSE WON'T GO LEFT.

But, incredibly, 1950 was to prove infinitely bigger for Colonist and for his owner, as well as underlining how typically involved Winston had become with his new activity. He was no Mr Toad, taking things up to quickly let them go. He seemed to have infinite space for a fresh enthusiasm, and all this at a time when he had shrunk Labour's lead in a February General Election and was continuing to work hard on his war memoirs.

Of course, dictating letters and articles is easier than writing them oneself, and Churchill dragged long-suffering secretaries wherever he went. But Winston made greater virtue of the dictating facility than anyone else in history, not least in the touchingly domestic 'Chartwell Bulletins' he sent Clemmie when, as was often the case, she was recuperating somewhere. The entry for 18 April 1950 shows how much horses and racing had come into the picture.

> *The little grey pony which is with* [the cows] *now comes when called, at a gallop, three or four hundred yards, to eat a piece of bread, a new feature in my daily peregrinations.*

> *The two filly foals* [he is still calling them foals from last year, but they are technically 'yearlings'] *are well and strong and will have to be broken soon. The brood mare Poetic went to Lord Derby's to have her foal, which is a colt with three white anklets and a white star, said to be very good-looking. He is by King Legend and may well be a valuable animal. Poetic will be married this week to Lord Derby's Borealis, and it is thought that this progeny will also be valuable. I may buy another broodmare with a colt foal in order to keep company with the new foal by Poetic.*

> *April 29 will be a big day for us. Colonist II runs in the 'Winston Churchill Stakes' at Hurst Park the same day that his sister runs*

for the first time there too. I hope you will come to see these two horses running. So far all this shows quite a substantial profit, and the whole outfit could be sold for two or three times what we gave for it. In addition there are twelve hundred pounds of winnings with Weatherbys [horseracing's official administrators]. *Of course I do not expect Colonist to win the 'Winston Churchill Stakes'. He will meet the best horses in the world there.*

Allowance must be made for exaggeration when Churchill writes 'best horses in the world'. But proof of how much higher Colonist was aiming lies in his 20-1 starting price, so second place behind the French winner Wild Mec was wholly admirable, and the galloping grey then embarked on a run of success which was little short of phenomenal.

In May he won at Kempton and Hurst Park before finishing a gallant fourth in the Ascot Gold Cup to the French horse Supertello, and then running up a sequence of victories at Sandown, Goodwood, Kempton and Ascot. The five-timer was set for the Lowther Stakes at Newmarket on 12 October, the day after Churchill had been elected a member of the Jockey Club, at the same time as he was in Copenhagen to receive an Honorary Doctorate at the university and Denmark's highest honour – the somewhat oriental-sounding Order Of The Elephant.

In the Newmarket race Colonist went to the front as usual, and although a 15-year-old Lester Piggott swept through to lead 150 yards from the line, Colonist thrust his way back to win on the post, causing John Hislop, one of the greatest of amateur rider / journalists, to write in that Sunday's *Observer*, 'He seems to have become imbued with the unshakeable determination of his owner, Mr Winston Churchill, so that he simply will not accept defeat.'

More immediately, Peter O'Sullevan, then just a sharp-eyed reporter, his velvety tones not yet familiar to the broadcasting world, left us a quite unforgettable picture in the next morning's *Daily Express*.

MAN OF 75 HAS A DAY OUT
What a man. What a horse. Winston Churchill, I mean. Colonist II, I mean. Well, look at them. Winston is 75. The day before yesterday he wrote a big speech and delivered it before 7,000 people. Yesterday he got into a plane and flew 500 miles from Denmark to London.

Then he got into another plane and flew 70 miles to Newmarket. And there Colonist II came into the story.

The horse is only four years old. But it is the Churchill type. It ran a mile and three quarters and won by a short head at the astonishing price of 11 to 8.

Astonishing because Colonist II keeps on winning at odds against, when everyone would expect him to be odds on. This horse has now won ten races for Mr Churchill – and the public – at nice prices the last five wins in a row. Eleven to eight. Such charitable fellows, these bookmakers.

Who backed the other runners in this race is a riddle, because everyone was clapping as the winner came in. Winston went to pat his horse.

He arrived from Denmark with the brim of his Homburg hat turned up, but now the brim was turned down. He looked as happy as a man could be who has backed a winner.

Colonist II, a 'wonder horse' if ever there was one, has an objection to standing still after being unsaddled. Once or twice after his victories Mr Churchill has to step round warily to pat the horse's nose.

So it was yesterday. The fact that Mr Churchill is now a member of the Jockey Club made no difference. Just one pat, then he had to dodge as the horse turned round.

After that Mr Churchill stepped into a plane for his third flight of the day – 170 miles to Lytham St Annes, near Blackpool.

Crowds were waiting there to cheer him. His hat brim was now turned up again. He gave the throng a grin, a wave of his cigar, and the V-sign.

What a man.

Then and now, owning racehorses is a risky dalliance for a politician, and his secretary Jo Sturdee was not the only one to tell Churchill that it might lose him votes in the upcoming General Election. But owning a successful horse on which ordinary punters win money leads to a sense of common ownership. Owning one that keeps winning makes it even better. But best of all is to have one that is grey, runs over long distances, and sets off in front to make the running. The most popular horse in all my time was the grey trailblazing steeplechaser Desert Orchid. In the 1940s and 1950s, the most popular was Colonist II. What a vote winner for a politician! While Churchill was heading for the Conservative party conference, the afternoon proceedings had been stopped to announce the result of the 3.15 at Newmarket, and the whole hall had burst out cheering.

WSC in the winners' enclosure
after Colonist II wins at Kempton
in September 1950

There was also plenty of cheer amongst Churchill's personal entourage, because he was both a bold punter and generous winner. In that Lowther Stakes he put on not only £300 (£8,000 in today's money) for himself, but also £10 for Clementine, £15 for Sergeant Williams, his Scotland Yard detective, and £2 for Miss Marston, one of the secretaries at Chartwell. 'In Victory – Magnanimity,' was one of Winston's epithets, along with that famous trio 'In War – Resolution', 'In Defeat – Defiance', and 'In Peace – Goodwill', and in May 1951 Churchill was even extending 'Magnanimity' to the Royal Family.

For Colonist II had scored a highly appropriate victory in the Winston Churchill Stakes at Hurst Park, beating King George VI's horse Above Board. The owner's thank-you letter to Princess Elizabeth is a little treasure:

> *Madam,*
>
> *I must thank Your Royal Highness for so kindly asking me to luncheon with you at Hurst Park on Saturday, and for the gracious compliments with which you honoured me. I wish indeed that we both could have been victorious – but that would have been no foundation for the excitements and liveliness of the Turf.*
>
> *Believe me Your Royal Highness' devoted servant*
> *Winston S. Churchill*

Bigger targets than even royal favour beckoned for both horse and owner. For Colonist the challenge was the two-and-a-half-mile Ascot Gold Cup, the most prestigious long-distance test in the world of Flat racing, and the pinnacle of the Royal Ascot meeting in June. For Churchill, it was to become Conservative Prime Minister once more at the next General Election. The sense in which these two targets were intertwined is caught perfectly by the entry in Harold Macmillan's diary for 14 June 1951, the morning of the Ascot Gold Cup. 'Conscious that many people feel that he is too old to form a government,' he writes of the 76-year-old leader,

> *and that this will probably be used as a cry against him at the election, he has used these days to give a demonstration of energy and vitality. He has voted in every division; made a series of brilliant little speeches; shown all his qualities of humour and sarcasm: and crowned all by a remarkable break-fast (at 7.30 a.m.) of eggs, bacon, sausages and coffee, followed by a large whisky and soda and a huge cigar. The latter fact commanded general admiration. He has been praised every day for all this by Lord Beaverbrook's papers; he has driven in and out of Palace Yard [in the Houses of Parliament] among*

groups of admiring and cheering sightseers, and altogether
nothing remains except for Colonist II to win the Gold Cup
this afternoon.

Colonist did not quite make it at Ascot – finishing a close second to the French horse Pan II – but on 26 October Churchill made it back to Number 10, by which time Colonist was destined to be sold as a stallion, his owner having declined to keep him with the now famous retort, 'To stud? And have it said that the Prime Minister of Great Britain is living off the immoral earnings of a horse?'

Far from being an electoral liability, racing in general and Colonist II in particular had turned into a huge political bonus. As a little boy growing up in London I remember the pictures in the papers and the images on the Pathé News of the famous old man that my father clearly revered: the Homburg hat, the cheering crowds, the V-for-Victory sign, and the gallant grey and his Scottish jockey Tommy Gosling setting off in front and defying the others to pass.

Colonist II and Tommy Gosling draw clear
in the White Rose Stakes at Hurst Park,
26 May 1961

16

SUNSET,
1952–1965

"Christopher is very clever about horses & the stud has become numerous and valuable: and pays for itself so far."

Colonist may have retired, and the ever-expanding pressure of government business may have returned, yet Churchill's involvement with horseracing not only continued but actually grew. In 1952 the 77-year-old Prime Minister had five horses in training: Pol Roger, Loving Cup, Non Stop, Gibraltar III and Prince Arthur, all of which won at least one race, a rare and enviable record for any owner. Although, unlike most of his other activities, Winston had almost entirely delegated the decision-making, he greatly enjoyed watching his horses run, and the vicarious pleasure of hearing about their progress when he could not make it. In his riding days he often appears to have given no more identity to a horse than we now do to a car, but with his racehorses he could hail success and bemoan failure almost as if they were family members.

Appearing at race meetings was now an applauded pleasure. On Saturday 6 June 1953 he was at Epsom to watch the Queen's horse Aureole run second in the Derby, four days after Her Majesty's coronation in Westminster Abbey. Three months later, Winston's attendance at Doncaster, when Aureole was third, although favourite, in the St Leger had rather more significance. It was to prove to himself, his family, his cabinet colleagues, his monarch and most of all the unwitting public that he was still capable of prime ministerial duties after secretly suffering a stroke a fortnight after the Derby, a drama vividly recreated for TV in 2015 in *Churchill's Secret*.

Not all Winston's colleagues were either convinced by or happy at his recovery. 'This simply cannot go on,' the Foreign Secretary, and Churchill's designated successor, Anthony Eden was writing by the end of March 1954: 'he is gaga; he cannot finish his sentences.' Yet, despite such exasperation, Churchill still had the energy, ambition and political cunning to last another 13 months in office, including a trip to Washington to meet President Eisenhower, and a secret agreement with the Defence Committee for Britain to build a hydrogen bomb. As ever, he would chronicle these forays in loving letters to Clementine which, despite her having told a friend that she did not find racing 'madly amusing', often included boyishly enthusiastic news of how his horses were doing.

In a long letter dictated in the car to and from Hurst Park on Saturday 5 June 1954, he tells how he had suspended the Cabinet Meeting at 12.30 on the Wednesday so as to get to the Derby (won by Lester Piggott on the appropriately named Never Say Die). It relates how, after a Downing Street meeting that Saturday morning with Anthony Eden, freshly back from the travails of the Geneva peace talks, he had raced off to watch Prince Arthur (son of that first mare Poetic) run a good third at Hurst Park. 'For one thrilling second a hundred yards from home,' the letter tells, 'he took the first place, he was third, but even that paid his expenses for a good many months.' Before signing off, Churchill added that he was going back to Hurst Park on the Tuesday to watch a horse called Pigeon Vole. He also had the time confidently to refute his wife's dietary advice in response to an obvious increase in poundage:

> *It says I am 14 stone and a half compared to the previous version of 15 stone on your machine and 15 stone and a half on the broken down one at Chartwell. The two in London are being tested on Tuesday next and if your machine is proved to be wrong you will have to review your conclusions, and I hope to abandon your regime. I have no grievance against a tomato, but I think one should eat other things as well.*

That weedy 31-inch-chest Sandhurst cadet belonged to another age.

WSC with a foal at the Newchapel Stud near Chartwell, which he bought in 1955

The old hero's actual resignation of the Premiership on 5 April 1955, at the age of 80, only increased the racing activity. Two months later, and there was even the first Churchill classic winner – albeit an Irish one – since Lord Randolph's L'Abbesse De Jouarre's Oaks back in 1889. The success was in the Irish 1,000 Guineas at the Curragh racecourse west of Dublin, with a filly called Dark Issue, leased from the owner by arrangement with the trainer's son Tim Rogers, who had made a big impression on Winston when seconded to him during his 'recovery' break on Lake Como after the shattering post-war election defeat. Churchill wasn't able to attend: he had resigned as Prime Minister, but not as an MP, and in May 1955 a vote at his Woodford seat was impending. 'The General Election was my owner,' he wrote in apology, 'and I was already entered among the runners.'

An even bigger story for the Churchill racing operation around this time was the purchase, for the improbably low price of £6,500, of the 80-acre, 26-box Newchapel Stud, not a dozen miles to the west of Chartwell. Another £1,000 a year brought in Arnold Carey Foster as stud and racing manager, and he and Christopher Soames then bought five mares as foundation stock for what was to prove a very successful enterprise that, within five years, would produce in Vienna and High Hat two of the best colts of their generation.

Meanwhile Winston would get much pleasure from Colonist II's half-brother Le Pretendant, who in 1956 won three races, and was so impressive when beating the Queen's High Veldt in the Cumberland Lodge Stakes at Ascot that the colt earned himself a trip to the Washington DC International, at what was to prove a hopelessly muddy Laurel Park in Maryland. Out there Le Pretendant did not appreciate the soft going any more than he had when flown to Düsseldorf four months earlier, and beat only one other finisher.

Churchill – a mere 81 – had flown there on a private plane with his loyal and long-suffering private secretary Anthony Montague Brown, and been given a huge reception and a slap-up lunch complete with champagne in huge glasses with a peach floating on top. Bumping about on the plane back, Winston grumbled to Montague Brown that the going was too soft and the peaches had ruined the champagne.

The pictures of Winston in the paddock with Le Pretendant show the increasingly static and distant figure of his closing years, but while visits to the racetrack began to become unlikely, pleasure at victory remained. 'What fun it was winning two races in one day!' he wrote from the south of France on news of a double at Windsor in June 1957. 'Quite an event for a beginner. Christopher is very clever about horses & the stud has become numerous and valuable: and pays for itself so far.' A year later celebrations of his and Clemmie's golden wedding down on the Riviera were enhanced by a telegram saying that the home-bred Welsh Abbot had won the ultra-competitive and much-coveted Portland Handicap at Doncaster.

By 1960 the light was fading. 'My life is over but it is not yet ended,' he told his daughter Diana in one dark moment. 'I love you so much, darling Papa,' Mary Soames wrote on 7 July with heartbreaking poignancy, 'and hate it that life should be such a poor, pale thing for you now.' How ironic that in this year and the next, Soames and Carey Foster's good stewardship paid its fullest dividends with the exploits of the brilliant and well-named colts Vienna, by Aureole out of Turkish blood, and High Hat, by Hyperion out of Madonna.

Churchill may have been increasingly immobile, and at times gloomy, but when Vienna put himself firmly in the picture for the Derby by winning the Blue Riband Trial Stakes on the Epsom track in April, *The Times* reported that 'There was a great cheer when Sir Winston Churchill came to the front of his box and waved to the crowd' and the paper went on to add 'Sir Winston now has two colts with prospects for the Derby as his High Hat ran promisingly in the 2,000 Guineas Trial Stakes at Kempton last Saturday.'

Sadly neither horse made it to the Derby. High Hat ran a good fifth in the 2,000 Guineas but was then sidelined until July. Vienna looked like being a major contender only to be injured while being shod on Derby morning. Ironically his significantly inferior stablemate Auroy finished fourth to the winner, St Paddy. Vienna went on to finish third in the St Leger, and to compete successfully in the highest company as a four- and five-year old.

High Hat winning the Winston Churchill Stakes at Hurst Park on 22 May 1961

High Hat was a matching, if slower-burning asset, only coming to his best as a four-year-old when he finished the season running fourth in the Prix de l'Arc de Triomphe at Longchamp, then being sold as a stallion to the Airlie Stud and Churchill's young Irish ally Tim Rogers. Vienna would join him there a year later. Earlier in the season, High Hat had run up a memorable hat-trick, including the Winston Churchill Stakes and the Aly Khan Memorial Stakes at Kempton, in which he defeated the star mare Petite Etoile, who had been owned by the late Aly himself.

Geoff Lewis rode both Vienna and High Hat in the summer of 1960, winning the Blue Riband on Vienna and being second at Kempton when High Hat reappeared in July. 'They were two cracking colts,' said Geoff Lewis looking back in August 2017, 'both of them were chestnuts, High Hat was a bit taller but Vienna gave me a great feel at Epsom and I think he would have gone really close in the Derby and might have won the St Leger if he hadn't pulled so hard. Sir Winston did not come down to meet him but to us he was a total legend.'

It was the highest of days for those in the Nightingall yard. 'I can't say that the old man was ever around the yard at this stage,' says the bloodstock adviser Julian Lewis, back then a callow young assistant at South Bank. 'But the Churchill aura was everywhere. Petite Etoile was a superstar, and for High Hat to go and beat her was something we would never forget.'

Vienna wins the Prix d'Harcourt in April 1962, WSC's only winner in France

By 1963 Lewis remembers High Hat's half-brother Sun Hat, also from the Churchill stable, as being more impressive on the gallops than anything the Nightingall team had ever had at Epsom, but so signally failing to transfer his morning form to the afternoons that he was shipped off to the Queen's trainer Peter Cazalet to go hurdling. This different challenge proved more suitable, and Sun Hat quickly won three races and started second favourite in the 1964 Champion Hurdle.

Churchill's concentration was now at a low ebb, but his sense of fun could still shine through. Sun Hat's jockey was a brilliant and saucy young South Londoner called David Mould, who one day, as requested, knocked on the front door of Chartwell, only to be turned away by the staff. The error corrected, he was led in awe to the study. The great man fixed him with a long, daunting stare before growling, 'So what are we going to give you as a present?'

Even then, Mould was not one to be easily flummoxed. Seeing some handsome boxes of Cuban cigars behind the desk, he pointed optimistically in their direction.

'Oh, no,' the famous voice rumbled, with a laugh that recalled his own chutzpah from so long ago. 'They are far too good for you.' And with a benign smile the old hero handed over a handsome cheque.

There would not be many more public sightings, although in July 1964 Churchill did make one last public appearance in the Commons. Then in November, three days before Winston's 90th birthday, a final thank you letter was sent on his behalf to Walter Nightingall.

My dear Nightingall,

It is very sad for me to have to end my racing activities owing to the fact that my health does not allow me to attend race meetings any more. I know that this decision will cause sorrow to you too, since we have had such a long association. My mind goes back to the spring of 1949, when Christopher persuaded me to buy Colonist. He gave us all great excitement and pleasure, and he was also the forerunner of many successes. I am so grateful to you for the skilful way in which you have trained the horses that I have sent to you from my stud. It does not fall to many people to start a racing career at the age of 75 and to reap from it such pleasure.

I send you my warm thanks for all that you have done, and my very best wishes.

Yours faithfully,
Winston S. Churchill

It was the close of a wonderful sunset activity. In 16 years Churchill had raced 46 horses and won 71 races, earning over £90,000 in prize-money, £120,000 in bloodstock sales and, much more importantly, an interest that Churchill took to his heart. Have a look at the picture of Winston handling one of his foals in the paddock, and think back through the days when the warrior Winston had horses galloping beneath him, all the way to that 15-year-old boy riding out from Banstead Manor with his father to watch L'Abbesse De Jouarre work on the Limekilns.

The challenge, the escape and the power that horses gave had been one of the shaping forces of his life, and should not be forgotten. They had given him courage and stature when they were most needed; they had carried him in the most perilous moments of his days; and they informed his words, his attitudes and his love of life.

After a massive stroke a fortnight earlier, Winston Churchill finally died on 24 January 1965, the same date as Lord Randolph had departed 70 years before. The funeral was on a freezing cold Saturday eight days later. I watched on TV at the Cotswold home of jockey David Nicholson as the State Barge processed mournfully up the Thames and we then set off to race over jumps at Windsor racetrack where in September 1949 Winston had first watched Colonist II.

I was two months away from riding in my first Grand National, with a head full of Will H. Ogilvie's line about Aintree, 'Danger beckons yet to daring', just as the young Churchill's had been with the imperial heroics of G.A. Henty and H.L. Rider Haggard. As a rider I was a bit more organised than he had been as a 20-year-old going out for the Subalterns' Cup, but with a lot less between my ears or achievements up ahead. Yet for both of us, horses were a means to an end and comrades too.

So much of his earlier life and final days involved them that the equestrian story deserves its place in the wider tale that never fades. For to follow in some of his hoofprints has been to realize that, even in the saddle, no one has ever traced quite as extraordinary a path as the horseman that was Winston Spencer Churchill.

WSC at Chartwell

INDEX

ACKNOWLEDGEMENTS

The map of Winston Churchill's life is so vast that any new traveller must ask for directions. These acknowledgements are but a small token of the thanks I owe to the many who have helped me along this journey and I crave forgiveness for those who I have somehow forgotten to mention. You were all wonderful.

Nicholas Soames was an unflagging ally from the very beginning when Sean Magee's opening idea of a book about Churchill's racehorses developed into a wider field and then into what these pages contain. Sean himself has been a source of support as he has with many other things on which we have worked together.

Nicholas's first and most important introduction was to Allen Packwood, the Director of the Churchill Archives Centre to whom I am hugely indebted for the interest he has taken and the kind words he has written. His staff in Cambridge and particularly Katherine Thomson, have been unfailingly helpful with my many queries and being granted online access to the archive lit up the project on a daily basis and to an extent I had not thought possible. Looking again at copies of the original letters between Winston and his parents, his wife and his friends, were an inspiration as well as a reminder that primary sources are always best.

To that end the compilations by his grand-daughter Celia Sandys, *From Winston with Love and Kisses*, and by his daughter Mary Soames, *Speaking for Themselves*, were invaluable along the road as of course were the *Companion Volumes* to Martin Gilbert's monumental official biography. I had also re-read many other brilliant works from William Manchester to Roy Jenkins to Boris Johnson but it was always to the letters in the *Companion Volumes* that I returned.

Obviously, I started by spending many happy hours at Blenheim which is now the most brilliantly run of stately homes and where John Holt and Karen Wiseman were immediately helpful. So too were the staff at Emo Park in Ireland which I visited thanks to the support of my trusted friend Des Leadon who once again read through reams of manuscript as the book developed. A year after Jacqueline O'Brien's death it is poignant to be paying tribute to her book, *Great Irish Houses and Castles,* in which the entry on Emo Park was just what was needed at that early stage.

At Newmarket, Prince Khalid Abdullah's racing manager, Teddy Grimthorpe, was a friendly aide in cementing the previously ignored fact that the happiest childhood base of 'The Greatest Briton' was also the birthplace and is now home to Frankel, this century's greatest racehorse. I am indebted to Sir Mark Prescott for use of the 'Heath House' picture and for his unparalleled knowledge of Newmarket now and then. Getting an image in one's mind of the teenage Churchill was much helped by pages of his cousin Shane Leslie's, *The End of a Chapter,* by his mother Jennie's *Reminiscences of Lady Randolph Churchill*, by his aunt Anita Leslie's *Jennie, The Mother of Winston Churchill* and, besides all the previously mentioned letters, by Celia and John Lee's book, *Winston and Jack.*

At Sandhurst, I was warmly received both by the adjutant, Peter Middlemiss, and the Curator, Anthony Morton, as I tried to picture the 'feeble framed' Churchill taking those first steps to manhood. Key to those had been early riding lessons with the Household Cavalry whose current commander, James Gaselee, was as warm and friendly as his father Nick used to be when we raced together in the 1960s. Peter Storer, the Curator of the Household Cavalry Archive, was terrific in getting the tireless Ted Land to dig out some priceless contemporary details, not least the unfortunate demise of riding instructor, Charles Burt, when his carriage horse bolted in Piccadilly. Today's riding supremo, Brian Rogers, is unlikely to meet such a fate and was good and informative company as he introduced me to present day recruits.

The delight in discovering that the Aldershot Races in which Churchill rode in a steeplechase was what I later knew as Tweseldown, was doubled by the map and details of the original course sent in by that masterly esoteric historian, Chris Pitt. Re-imagining the galloping young subaltern was much helped by the pages of David Scott Daniell's definitive *Fourth Hussar* and by the present-day subaltern, Barnaby Spink, who rifled the regimental library to help. In all this and through all Churchill's young life, my particular quest would have been impossible without the relentless scholarship and supportive emails from Douglas Russell, whose book, *Winston Churchill, Soldier,* I found an invaluable, in depth and unbiased resource.

I hope I have acknowledged this in the text as I have also tried to do with Hal Klepak in appreciation of what he did for me in Cuba and for his book, *Churchill Comes of Age.* The week I spent travelling the island with him and the belief he had in the project changed the scope of this book and hugely energized my efforts to justify his welcome.

This certainly applied when it came to the North-West frontier and no re-imagining would have been possible without the pages and the counsel of Con Coughlin and his book, *Churchill's First War*.

The standard biographies give a good picture of India in the 1890s but I much enjoyed the often-apposite military and riding anecdotes in Hubert Gough's *Soldiering On* and the nonagenarian Sir Bindon Blood's splendid *Four Score Years and Ten*. Happiest find of all was the Kindle edition of Baden Powell's *Memories of India* which came complete with excellent line drawings a couple of which have been introduced earlier.

When it comes to Omdurman nothing could be done without a trip to see Mick Holtby at The Queen's Royal Lancers and Nottinghamshire Yeomanry Museum in Thoresby Park and then a deep immersion in his friend and colleague Terry Brighton's magnificent and encyclopaedic book, *The Last Charge*. One of the best memories of this whole operation has been standing on the Kerreri Hills watching the British Ambassador Michael Aron looking south over the Omdurman battlefield with Terry's book in hand for constant reference. I was privileged to have such a great Arabist as Michael to make things possible even if we did have a few quite uncomfortable moments when some heavily armed Sudanese police took a dim view of us peering out at what is now partly a site of a military base.

The Sudan trip only happened thanks to the good offices of Samia Omar and her husband, Osama Daoud. It was great to visit the Khartoum International Community School of which Samia has been so central a part and where this February, Jill Elllis and David Hancock ran the riding school alongside the river Nile. They also gave me bed and board and mounted me for a memorable ride along the route which Churchill would have taken at Omdurman. Favours don't come much bigger than that but Michael Aron's former Foreign Office colleague Bill Ridout came close with his tutorial on Sudanese history and his own adventures in the Swat Valley.

Our ride was somewhat more sedentary than that undertaken by Churchill 119 years before, but recapturing what the original must have been like was hugely assisted by the counsel of someone who took part in it, or rather in the *Young Winston* version back in 1972, himself. Vic Armstrong is a legend in his own right, not for nothing did Steven Spielberg dub him, 'The World's Greatest Stuntman', and for the film Vic trained both the horses and the actors and often rode as body double for the lead Simon Ward. There was the pleasantest of justifications for this project when I showed Vic the photo of the 71-year old Churchill cantering the Lipizzaner Salve in 1946 and he said, '*that man can ride*'.

Of course, Churchill himself is the best witness to his younger days when, as a working correspondent he showed a speed and quality of output that still makes most of us green with envy. This is especially so in India, Sudan and South Africa, and for the last named, I was lucky to have made a research trip some 15 years ago to Spion Kop where the horses and knowledge imparted by Jennifer Russell and the hospitality by Bill Bentley at his Rolling M Ranch still glow in the memory, as does the help of my friend, John Doble, then head of the British legation in Johannesburg.

When it came to Polo in India and nearer home, I had the great pleasure of being able to meet Reggie Hoare's grandson Toddy Hoare and share his memories. After that, I was in good hands with Simon Tomlinson who effortlessly handled my first call in the middle of the night from the yacht he was on in Thailand. He put me on to David Wood at Hurlingham and my path was eased by all the knowledge in Horace Laffaye's *Polo in Britain* and the vivid experience in Ted Miller's *Fifty Years of Sport*. Best of all the Hay Festival's legendary chair, Revel Guest, daughter of Churchill's 10-goal cousin Oscar Guest, put me in touch with Robert Young who dug out all sorts of fascinating details about Polo at the turn and early in the century.

For hunting Churchill's great-grandson Arthur Soames was an informed and enthusiastic aide and I was lucky enough to have an inspiring overnight stay in Rutland with Joss Hanbury, the fabled and long serving master of the Quorn. Top bloodstock agent and former master of the Cottesmore, Charlie Gordon-Watson was a big help as were the works of Michael Clayton and two wonderfully dated volumes, *Memories of The Shires* by John Otho Paget and *The Sport of Our Ancestors* by Lord Willoughby de Broke. But the diamond amongst all this was the hunting diary of the arch Tory Lord North unearthed by Clive Preston to whose introduction I am hugely grateful to my cousin, Sally Nicholson.

As to post war hunting, Annie Cairns is the expert on all things Surrey and Burstow, and Wizzie Hawksfield, John Dunlop, Nonie Chapman and Penny Carver were all instrumental in building up a picture of the late 1940s.

When it came to Churchill and the Yeomanry I struck lucky in finding an old friend in John Bridgeman as chairman of the Oxfordshire Soldiers Museum in Woodstock where he and his team and I spent the most enjoyable of afternoons digging up all sorts of nuggets of Edwardiana. One of the greatest pleasures of a Churchill quest is the places you visit and what is true of Blenheim, is in its smaller but more direct way, even more true of Chartwell. My trips there were inspirational, particularly with the image of Lord Randolph's ghost in the 1947 short story, *The Dream*, and with the idea of Winston wanting to recreate his father's life on the turf. It is said that Churchill's 90th birthday cake was iced out in the chocolate and pink of his racing colours. For help in that area Sean Magee's work was a perfect introduction and Fred Glueckstein's *Churchill and Colonist II* was a unique study of the horse to which racing owes Churchill's rekindled enthusiasm.

But beyond measure in resource was Tim Cox's library near Dorking, the closeness of which to my home has been one of the greatest of geographical blessings. Not only does Tim possess every racing reference publication imaginable, he himself is a studious perfectionist who, quite unprompted, produced a detailed horse-by-horse, race-by-race, guide to Churchill's fortunes on the turf. Talking of fortune, no mention of money and 'The Greatest Briton' can be complete without adding David Lough's *No More Champagne* from which I have borrowed any financial comparisons as the Churchill years have rolled by.

I had never worked with editor Graham Coster before but I very much hope to do so again. Because he can enthuse and challenge you at the same time, and debates on the manuscript became both a creative and a pleasurable process. When it was all over we had in Ian Greensill, a proof reader, who had high quality racing as well as professional connections.

Producing this volume has been quite an adventure for *Racing Post*. I am grateful to the paper's chief executive, Alan Byrne, and editor, Bruce Millington, for their forbearance, and for CFO Mark Francis for accepting our belief. Publisher Julian Brown has battled us through a few storms and James Norris has been an inventive quarrier of illustrations. We hit the jackpot when John Schwartz's excellent Soapbox design operation put the super talented Rachel Bray on our case and we lucked out again in finding Flora Blackett to step in and do such an evocative sketch for the cover illustration.

But none of this would have been possible without the diminutive life force that is Liz Ampairee. When others falter, she fastens on. When the pace quickens, so does she. In the inevitably stress filled closing stages she suffered the agony of family bereavement but still got us over the line. I just hope this book goes some way to justify her efforts.

Closer to home I am lucky in having Chris Elston as a neighbour with his own library of Churchill books, Pippa Heaton was a reassuring reader of unedited chapters and my PA Gill Heaney was the most generous of listeners as I gave her the audio version once each section was finished. Thanks to all my children and especially to my publisher son, Charlie, whose advice is ever perceptive even if nowadays it comes all the way from Dubai.

Finally, apologies to my wife Susie who has had to live through a year with Churchill, and what seemed like a thousand books all over the house. For me this project has been one of the most thrilling and fulfilling that I have ever done but I am aware of the hassle such obsessions bring in their wake. That is what's good about crossing the finishing line. We've made it. **BS**

PICTURE CREDITS